■ ALGONQUIN AREA PUBLIC LIBRARY DISTRICT

3 1488 00580 5635

Apr. 2013

■ SCHOL

OCTOBER
Monthly Idea Book

Ready-to-Use Templates, Activities, Management Tools, and More — for Every Day of the Month

Karen Sevaly

S0-AEI-618

Algonquin Area Public Library
2600 Harnish Dr.
Algonquin, IL 60102
www.aapld.org

New York • Toronto • London • Auckland • Sydney
Mexico City • New Delhi • Hong Kong • Buenos Aires

Teaching *Resources*

DEDICATION
This book is dedicated to teachers and children everywhere.

Scholastic Inc. grants teachers permission to photocopy the reproducible pages from this book for classroom use. No other part of this publication may be reproduced in whole or in part, or stored in a retrieval system, or transmitted in any form or by any means, electronic, mechanical, photocopying, recording, or otherwise, without permission of the publisher. For information regarding permission, write to Scholastic Inc., 557 Broadway, New York, NY 10012.

Cover design by Maria Lilja
Cover art by Jillian Phillips
Interior design by Melinda Belter
Illustrations by Karen Sevaly

ISBN 978-0-545-37934-2

Text and illustrations © 2013 by Scholastic Inc.
All rights reserved.
Printed in the U.S.A.

1 2 3 4 5 6 7 8 9 10   40   19 18 17 16 15 14 13

CONTENTS

FAVORITE TOPICS

CONTENTS

COLUMBUS DAY

FIRE SAFETY

DINOSAURS

Reproducible Patterns

SPIDERS AND OWLS

Reproducible Patterns

CONTENTS

SKELETONS

HALLOWEEN

AWARDS, INCENTIVES, AND MORE

Reproducible Patterns

ANSWER KEY

INTRODUCTION

Welcome to the original Monthly Idea Book series! This book was written especially for teachers getting ready to teach topics related to the month of October.

Each book in this month-by-month series is filled with dozens of ideas for PreK–3 classrooms. Activities connect to the Common Core State Standards for Reading (Foundational Skills), among other subjects, to help you meet the needs of your students. (For more information, see page 16.)

Most everything you need to prepare the lessons and activities in this resource is included, such as:

- calendar and weather-related props

- book cover patterns and stationery for writing assignments

- booklet patterns

- games and puzzles that support learning in curriculum areas such as math, science, and writing

- activity sheets that help students organize information, respond to learning, and explore topics in a meaningful way

- patterns for projects that connect to holidays, special occasions, and commemorative events

All year long, you can weave the ideas and reproducible patterns in these unique books into your monthly lesson plans and classroom activities. Happy teaching!

What's Inside

You'll find that this book is
chockfull of reproducibles
that make lesson planning easier:

- puppets and
picture props

- bookmarks, booklets,
and book covers

- game boards, puzzles,
and word finds

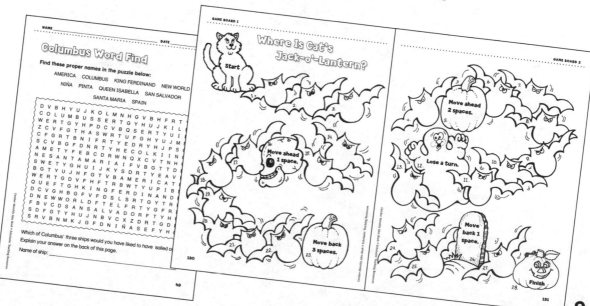

■ stationery

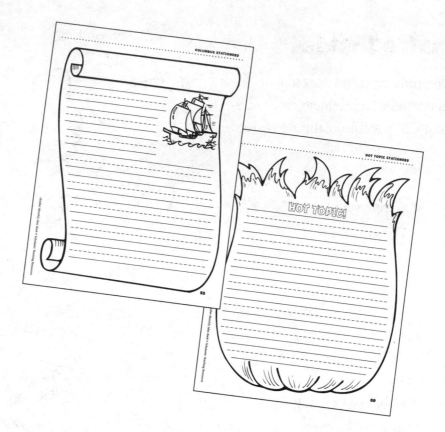

■ awards and certificates

How to Use This Book

The reproducible pages in this book have flexible use and may be modified to meet your particular classroom needs. Use the reproducible activity pages and patterns in conjunction with the suggested activities provided or weave them into your curriculum in other ways.

★ PHOTOCOPY OR SCAN

To get started, think about your developing lesson plans and upcoming bulletin boards. If desired, carefully remove the pages you will need. Duplicate those pages on copy paper, color paper, tagboard, or overhead transparency sheets. If you have access to a scanner, consider saving the pattern pages as PDF files. That way you can size images up or down and customize them with text to create individualized lessons, center-time activities, interactive whiteboard lessons, homework pages, and more.

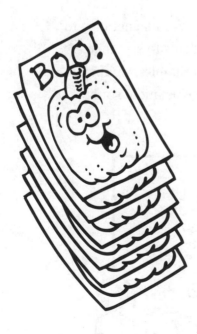

LAMINATE FOR DURABILITY

Laminating the reproducibles will help you extend their use. If you have access to a roll laminator, then you already know how fortunate you are when it comes to saving time and resources. If you don't have a laminator, clear adhesive vinyl covering works well. Just sandwich the pattern between two sheets of vinyl and cut off any excess. Then try some of these ideas:

■ Put laminated sheets of stationery in a writing center to use for handwriting practice. Wipe-off markers work great on coated pages and can easily be erased with dry tissue.

■ Add longevity to calendars, weather-related pictures, and pocket chart rebus pictures by preserving them with lamination.

■ Transform picture props into flannel board figures. After lamination, add a tab of hook-and-loop fastener to the back of the props and invite students to adhere them to the flannel board for storytelling fun.

■ To enliven magnet board activities, affix sections of magnet tape to the back of picture props. Then encourage students to sort images according to the skills you're working on. For example, you might have them group images by commonalities such as initial sound, habitat, or physical attributes.

BULLETIN BOARDS

1. Set the Stage

Use background paper colors that complement many themes and seasons. For example, the dark background you use as a spooky display in October will have dramatic effect in November, when you begin a unit on woodland animals or Thanksgiving.

While paper works well, there are other background options available. You might also try fabric from a colorful bed sheet or gingham material. Discontinued rolls of patterned wallpaper can be purchased at discount stores. What's more, newspapers are easy to use and readily available. Attach a background of comics to set off a lesson on riddles, or use grocery store flyers to provide food for thought on a bulletin board about nutrition.

2. Make the Display

The reproducible patterns in this book can be enlarged to fit your needs. When we say enlarge, we mean it! Think BIG! Use an overhead projector to enlarge the images you need to make your bulletin board extraordinary.

If your school has a stencil press, you're lucky. The rest of us can use these strategies for making headers and titles.

- Cut strips of paper, cloud shapes, or cartoon bubbles. They will all look great! Then, by hand, write the text using wide-tipped permanent markers or tempera paint.

- If you must cut individual letters, use 4- by 6-inch pieces of construction paper. (Laminate first, if you can.) Cut the uppercase letters as shown on page 14. No need to measure, as somewhat irregular letters will look creative, not messy.

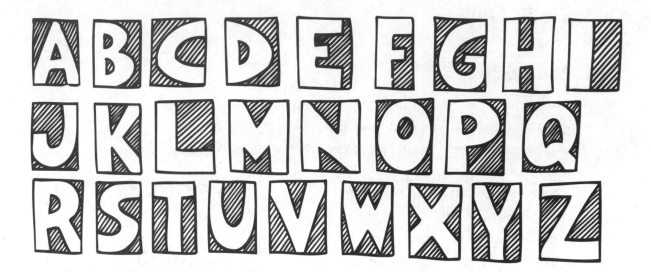

3. Add Color and Embellishments

Use your imagination! You'll be surprised at the great displays you can create.

- ■ Watercolor markers work great on small areas. On larger areas, you can switch to crayons, color chalk, or pastels. (Lamination will keep the color off of you. No laminator? A little hairspray will do the trick as a fixative.)

- ■ Cut character eyes and teeth from white paper and glue them in place. The features will really stand out and make your bulletin boards engaging.

- ■ For special effects, include items that provide texture and visual interest, such as buttons, yarn, and lace. Try cellophane or blue glitter glue on water scenes. Consider using metallic wrapping paper or aluminum foil to add a bit of shimmer to stars and belt buckles.

- ■ Finally, take a picture of your completed bulletin board. Store the photos in a recipe box or large sturdy envelope. Next year when you want to create the same display, you'll know right where everything goes. You might even want to supply students with pushpins and invite them to recreate the display, following your directions and using the photograph as support.

Staying Organized

Organizing materials with monthly file folders provides
you with a location to save reproducible activity pages and
patterns, along with related craft ideas, recipes, and magazine
or periodical articles.

If you prefer, use file boxes instead of folders. You'll find
that with boxes there will plenty of room to store enlarged
patterns, sample art projects, bulletin board materials, and
much more.

Meeting the Standards

CONNECTIONS TO THE COMMON CORE STATE STANDARDS

The Common Core State Standards Initiative (CCSSI) has outlined learning expectations in English/Language Arts, among other subject areas, for students at different grade levels. In general, the activities in this book align with the following standards for students in grades K–3. For more information, visit the CCSSI website at www.corestandards.org.

Reading: Foundational Skills

Print Concepts

• RF.K.1, RF.1.1. Demonstrate understanding of the organization and basic features of print.

Phonics and Word Recognition

• RF.K.3, RF.1.3, RF.2.3, RF.3.3. Know and apply grade-level phonics and word analysis skills in decoding words.

Fluency

• RF.K.4. Read emergent-reader texts with purpose and understanding.

• RF.1.4, RF.2.4, RF.3.4. Read with sufficient accuracy and fluency to support comprehension.

Writing

Production and Distribution of Writing

• W.3.4. Produce writing in which the development and organization are appropriate to task and purpose.

• W.K.5, W.1.5, W.2.5, W.3.5. Focus on a topic and strengthen writing as needed by revising and editing.

Research to Build and Present Knowledge

• W.K.7, W.1.7, W.2.7. Participate in shared research and writing projects.

• W.3.7. Conduct short research projects that build knowledge about a topic.

• W.K.8, W.1.8, W.2.8, W.3.8. Recall information from experiences or gather information from provided sources to answer a question.

Range of Writing

• W.3.10. Write routinely over extended time frames (time for research, reflection, and revision) and shorter time frames (a single sitting or a day or two) for a range of discipline-specific tasks, purposes, and audiences.

Speaking & Listening

Comprehension and Collaboration

• SL.K.1, SL.1.1, SL.2.1. Participate in collaborative conversations with diverse partners about grade-level topics and texts with peers and adults in small and larger groups.

• SL.K.2, SL.1.2, SL.2.2, SL.3.2. Recount or describe key ideas or details from a text read aloud or information presented orally or through other media.

• SL.K.3, SL.1.3, SL.2.3, SL.3.3. Ask and answer questions about what a speaker says in order to gather additional information or clarify something that is not understood.

Presentation of Knowledge and Ideas

• SL.K.4, SL.1.4, SL.2.4. Describe people, places, things, and events with relevant details, expressing ideas and feelings clearly.

• SL.K.5, SL.1.5, SL.2.5, SL.3.5. Add drawings or other visual displays to stories or recounts of experiences when appropriate to clarify ideas, thoughts, and feelings.

Language

Conventions of Standard English

• L.K.1, L.1.1, L.2.1, L.3.1. Demonstrate command of the conventions of standard English grammar and usage when writing or speaking.

• L.K.2, L.1.2, L.2.2, L.3.2. Demonstrate command of the conventions of standard English capitalization, punctuation, and spelling when writing.

Knowledge of Language

• L.2.3, L.3.3. Use knowledge of language and its conventions when writing, speaking, reading, or listening.

Vocabulary Acquisition and Use

• L.K.4, L.1.4, L.2.4, L.3.4. Determine or clarify the meaning of unknown and multiple-meaning words and phrases based on grade level reading and content, choosing flexibly from an array of strategies.

• L.K.6, L.1.6, L.2.6, L.3.6. Use words and phrases acquired through conversations, reading and being read to, and responding to texts.

CALENDAR TIME

Getting Started

October Monthly Ideas • Scholastic Teaching Resources

October

Sunday	Monday	Tuesday	Wednesday	Thursday	Friday	Saturday

19

CALENDAR

★ MARK YOUR CALENDAR

Make photocopies of the calendar grid on page 19 and use it to meet your needs. Consider using the write-on spaces to:

- write the corresponding numerals for each day

- mark and count how many days have passed

- track the weather with stamps or stickers

- note student birthdays

- record homework assignments

- communicate with families about positive behaviors

- remind volunteers about schedules, field trips, shortened days, and so on

★ CELEBRATIONS THIS MONTH

Whether you post a photocopy of pages 20 though 23 near your class calendar or just turn to these pages for inspiration, you're sure to find lots of information on them to discuss with students. To take celebrating and learning a step further, invite the class to add more to the list. For example, students can add anniversaries of significant events and the birthdays of their favorite authors or historical figures.

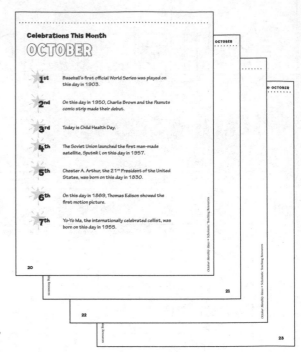

★ CALENDAR HEADER

You can make a photocopy of the header on page 24, color it, and use it as a title for your classroom calendar. You might opt to give the coloring job to a student who has a birthday that month. The student is sure to enjoy seeing his or her artwork each and every day of the month.

★ BEFORE INTRODUCING WHAT'S THE WEATHER?

Make a photocopy of the body template on page 25. Laminate it so you can use it again and again. Before sharing the template with the class, cut out pieces of cloth in the shapes of clothing students typically wear this month. For example, if you live in a warm weather climate, your October attire might include shorts and t-shirts. If you live in chillier climates, your attire might include a scarf, hat, and coat. Fit the cutouts to the body outline. When the clothing props are made, and you're ready to have students dress the template, display the clothing. Invite the "weather helper of the day" to tell what pieces of clothing he or she would choose to dress appropriately for the weather. (For extra fun, use foam to cut out accessories such as an umbrella, sunhat, and raincoat.)

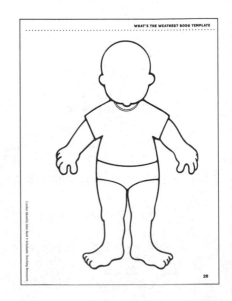

October

Sunday	Monday	Tuesday	Wednesday	Thursday	Friday	Saturday

Celebrations This Month

OCTOBER

 1st Baseball's first official World Series was played on this day in 1903.

 2nd On this day in 1950, Charlie Brown and the *Peanuts* comic strip made their debut.

 3rd Today is Child Health Day.

 4th The Soviet Union launched the first man-made satellite, *Sputnik I*, on this day in 1957.

 5th Chester A. Arthur, the 21st President of the United States, was born on this day in 1830.

 6th On this day in 1889, Thomas Edison showed the first motion picture.

 7th Yo-Yo Ma, the internationally celebrated cellist, was born on this day in 1955.

8th On this day in 1871, the Great Fire of Chicago broke out. The fire destroyed more than 17,000 buildings, took about 300 lives, and left 90,000 people homeless.

9th The Washington Monument officially opened to the public on this day in 1888.

10th The 1831 London Bridge was purchased by an American in 1968, reassembled in Arizona, and opened on this day in 1971.

11th Eleanor Roosevelt, American first lady and humanitarian, was born on this day in 1884.

12th On this day in 1492, Christopher Columbus first sighted land in what is now know as the Americas.

13th The United States Navy was established on this day in 1775.

14th On this day in 1964, Dr. Martin Luther King, Jr., was awarded the Nobel Peace Prize.

15th Congress established the Department of Transportation on this day in 1966.

16th Noah Webster, creator of the American dictionary, was born on this day in 1758.

17th On this day in 1711, Jupiter Hammon, the first African-American poet to be published, was born.

18th American inventor Samuel Morse laid the first telegraph cable on this day in 1842.

19th Today is Yorktown Day. In 1781, the last battle of the Revolutionary War was fought in Yorktown, Virginia.

20th On this day in 1910, a baseball with a cork center was used for the first time in a World Series game.

21st Alfred Bernhard Nobel, originator of the Nobel Prizes and inventor of dynamite, was born on this day in 1833.

22nd Thomas Alva Edison successfully tested the first electric light on this day in 1879. It glowed for 13 ½ hours before going out.

23rd John Heisman, the famous football, basketball, and baseball player and coach, was born on this day in 1869. Football's Heisman Trophy was named after him.

24th The United Nations was officially chartered on this day in 1945.

25th Richard Byrd, famous American polar explorer, was born on this day in 1888.

26th The First Continental Congress adjourned on this day in 1774.

27th The 26th President of the United States, Theodore Roosevelt, was born on this day in 1858.

28th On this day in 1886, a dedication ceremony was held for The Statue of Liberty—a gift from the people of France to the United States.

29th The International Red Cross was founded in Geneva, Switzerland, on October 29, 1863.

30th John Adams, one of the Founding Fathers and second President of the United States, was born on this day in 1735.

31st Today is Halloween!

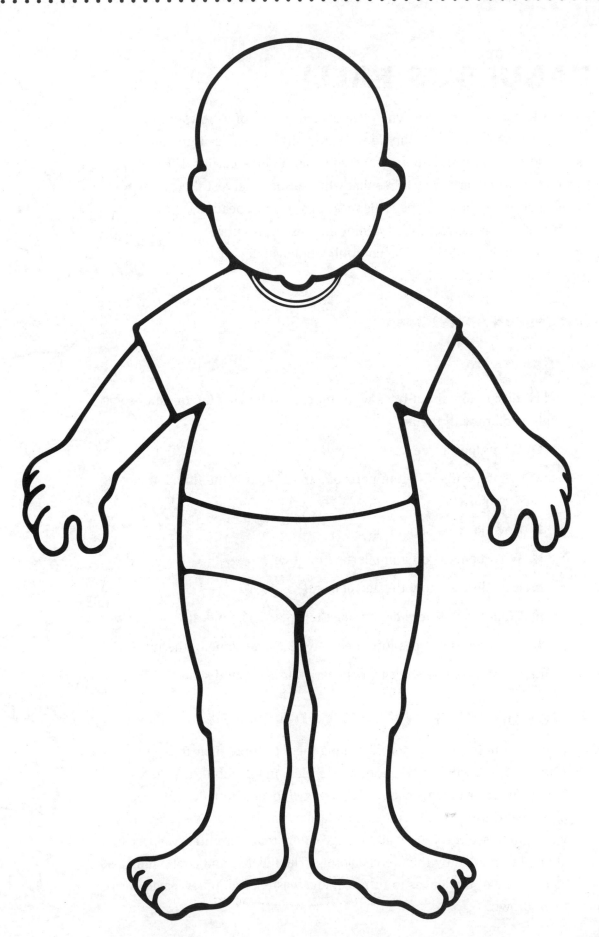

FABULOUS FALL!

Fall marks that time of year when leaves turn shades of yellow, orange, and red before falling from the trees. Wind twirls the leaves through the air as its sudden chill warns that winter is just around the corner. The sun begins to set earlier each evening while farmers harvest their fields of corn and other crops. This magical season of beauty and bounty is the perfect time to enjoy and discover nature. Help open students' eyes to the colorful, fabulous fall season with these activities.

Suggested Activities

 TREE TALK

Hold a discussion about trees with students. Following are questions you might explore with them:

- What does a tree need to grow?
- What are the different parts of a tree? What is the function of each part?
- How do trees benefit us?
- What benefits do animals get from trees?
- How do we know the age of trees?
- What type of trees are among the largest? The oldest?
- What types of trees lose their leaves? Name some of these trees.
- What trees lose their leaves near your home and school?

 WHY DO LEAVES CHANGE COLORS?

Pose this question to students, inviting them to share their thoughts. Afterward, use this explanation to help them understand the process: The green color in leaves, called *chlorophyll*, begins to fade and disappear during the shorter, cooler days of fall. As the green goes away, we begin to see the yellow and orange colors that were in the leaves all along, but hidden by the green coloring. The fall sun and cool nights also cause some of the leaves to turn red, and waste left in other leaves turns them brown.

ADOPT-A-TREE

As students watch trees shed their leaves, invite them to select a tree to observe year-round. This could be a tree in their yard at home, one at school, or one in the community that they frequently encounter. Have students make a scrapbook to document the changes in their adopted tree throughout the year. They might include a drawing or photograph of their tree, the name of the tree, a description that may even include observations about its height and trunk diameter, and a rubbing of its bark. Also, as leaves or blooms fall, they might press these between waxed paper and add them to their scrapbook. If students notice that animals, birds, or other critters use the tree as a home, have them record this information in their books, too. They might even snap pictures to add to their books! Each week, remind students to update the information on their tree and record their observations. Periodically, invite them to share about their tree with the class.

LOOKING AT LEAVES

Collect a supply of fallen leaves. Try to get leaves from different kinds of trees. In class, distribute the leaves, then draw a large leaf outline on the chalkboard. Add one part of the leaf at a time to your drawing (see below), naming and labeling each part as you go. Finally, point out each part on an actual leaf. Have students examine their leaves to find the corresponding part.

> **blade:** the broad part of the leaf that contains the food-making cells
>
> **veins:** a network of tiny tubes that move food through the leaf
>
> **petiole (leafstalk):** a stalk that carries food from the leaf to the tree

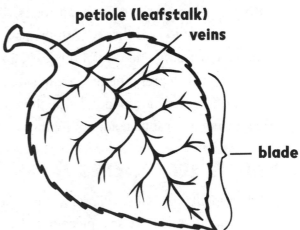

LEAF EXPLORATIONS

Take students on a nature walk to find colorful leaves that have fallen from different kinds of trees. Then invite them to make additional leaf discoveries with these creative activities.

Lasting Leaves

Help students preserve their finds by pressing the leaves between sheets of waxed paper. To do this, lay several thicknesses of newspaper on a table. Place the leaves between two sheets of waxed paper, set on the newspaper, and cover with more newspaper. Then press with a warm iron to seal the leaves between the waxed paper. (As an alternative, you might laminate the leaves.) To display, use yarn or nylon thread to suspend the pressed leaves in a sunny window for everyone to enjoy.

Leaf Rubbings

Ask each student to place a leaf on a flat surface, such as a table, and then cover it with a sheet of drawing paper. Have them gently rub the side of a crayon across the paper, pressing just enough to make an impression of the leaf under the paper. If desired, students can use several fall colors for their leaf rubbings, overlapping the colors to create an interesting effect. Use students' leaf rubbings to create a class bulletin board, or invite them to use their artwork as a cover for their fall-related writings.

Leaf Prints

Mix tempera paint in several fall colors. Then have students choose a leaf to coat lightly with the paint color of their choice (coat only one side of the leaf). To make a leaf print, ask students to press the leaf, paint side down, onto a large sheet of construction paper. Invite them to repeat, making leaf prints in various colors to fill their page.

★ SUNNY LEAF SHAPES

Ask students to choose a large leaf to tape to the center of a piece of red construction paper. (Use a piece of rolled tape on the back of the leaf.) Have them place their papers on a windowsill or other area that receives direct sunlight. After a few days, have students remove their leaf to reveal its outline on the paper. Talk about how the print was created (light from the sun faded the paper around the leaf, but not under the leaf).

★ LEAFY TREES

Distribute copies of the tree pattern (page 34) for students to color and cut out. Invite them to glue on torn tissue-paper leaves to create a colorful fall tree. After students complete their trees, help them brainstorm words that describe fall trees. Write each word on a plain index card. Display the trees and word cards on a bulletin board.

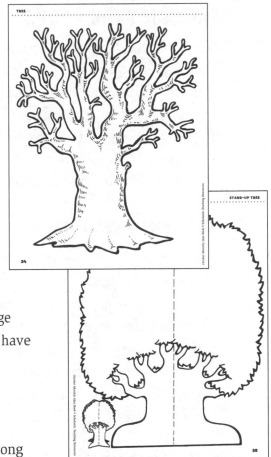

More advanced students might create a stand-up tree instead. To begin, copy the stand-up tree pattern (page 35) onto tagboard. Make two copies for each child. Then have students follow these directions to construct their tree:

1. Color and cut out both patterns.

2. Fold each tree on the dashed line, then unfold.

3. Align the trees back-to-back and staple together along the folds.

4. Pull the sides of one tree forward and the other tree back, and stand it on a flat surface.

5. Glue small pieces of red, yellow and orange tissue paper to all sides of the treetop.

To create a fall forest, place the stand-up trees on a table. If desired, add word cards, folded in half "tent-style" so they stand upright.

★ FALL-INSPIRED WRITING

Liven up writing assignments about fall by providing students with the leaf book cover (page 36) and stationery (page 37). Encourage them to write about changes that happen to trees and leaves in the fall, animal activity during the season, fall weather, or any other fall-related topic. Students can staple their pages to the cover when finished, then share their writing with classmates.

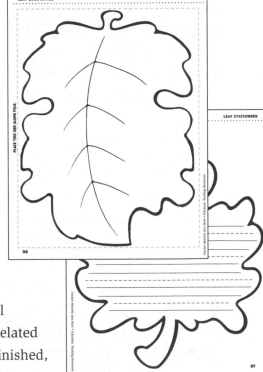

★ FALL PICTURE PROPS

Copy, color, and cut out the patterns on page 38. You can use these in numerous ways, such as for name tags, calendar symbols, word walls, flash cards, patterning practice, or matching activities. Or, you might use an overhead projector to trace large images of the patterns onto poster board or bulletin board paper. Color, cut out, and use the images to create displays or signs to post around the room.

★ AUTUMN AWARDS!

Display a large, bare tree made from brown butcher paper. Then cut out a supply of the leaf patterns (page 38) in various fall colors, such as red, yellow, and orange. Put the cutouts in a basket and place near the tree. Then use the display to award students when they complete assignments, exhibit improved behavior, or meet specific goals. Simply write the child's name, date, and accomplishment on a leaf. Then present the leaf to the child and help him or her attach it to the tree. Title the display "Autumn Awards!"

★ A FLURRY OF FINE WORK

Highlight student work along with the bright colors of fall with this bulletin board idea. Simply arrange colorful fall leaves on the display so they appear to be swirling, drifting, and curving in the air. (If desired, laminate the leaves.) Or, copy and cut out a supply of the leaf patterns on page 38 to display. Add student work and the title of this activity to the complete the display.

★ ACORNS AWAY!

Leaves aren't the only things that fall from trees—oak trees also drop acorns. Tell students that an acorn, or oak nut, is actually a seed. Many animals, such as squirrels, mice, birds, bears, and deer rely on acorn nuts as a source of food. When an acorn gets planted, it may germinate and eventually grow into a large oak tree. After sharing, ask students to research acorns and oak trees to learn more. Invite them to write facts and other interesting information that they discover on enlarged cutouts of the acorn pattern (page 38). Display the acorns below a large tree display crafted from twisted bulletin board paper.

An acorn has a seed in its shell.

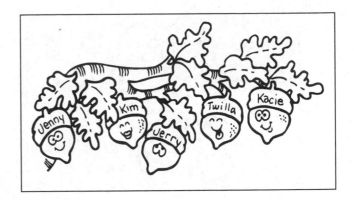

⭐ NUTS ABOUT FALL

Add some silliness to your fall studies with this idea. Give students a copy of the acorn pattern on page 38. Invite them to convert their acorn into silly faces or creatures. Provide colored markers and small craft items they can use to decorate their acorns. When finished, hang the acorn "nuts" from a paper tree branch displayed on a bulletin board.

⭐ CORNY EARS

In late summer and fall, many farmers set to work harvesting their corn crops. Explain that corn is an important food source for both people and animals. Bring in a few ears of corn to show students. Point out the different parts (described below), peeling back the husk and removing the silk to reveal the kernels, as needed. After sharing, provide students with a supply of craft materials, and invite them to create their own ears of corn. Encourage them to label the different parts on their completed work.

ear (or cob): the head, or top part, of a corn plant

kernels: the corn seeds that grow on the head and are used for food

husk: the leaves that wrap around and cover the ear of corn

silk: long, soft threads found inside the husk and extending from the top of the ear

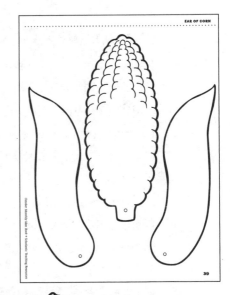

⭐ HARVEST THE FACTS

Liven up your classroom with a ready-to-pick cornfield! First, cut out a supply of the corn patterns on page 39. Copy the husk patterns on green paper and the corn on yellow. Label each pair of husks with a math fact, as shown. Write the answer on the corncob. Then use a brass fastener to assemble each ear of corn. Assemble your cornfield on a bulletin board, using construction-paper corn stalks. Invite students to practice their math facts by opening the ears of corn to check their answers.

⭐ HELLO, SCARECROW!

No cornfield is complete without
a friendly scarecrow standing watch over it. Invite
students to make their own scarecrow to display
with their fall writings. Distribute copies of pages 40–42 for
students to color and cut out. Then help them assemble their scarecrows, as
shown, using five brass fasteners. If desired, students can create a fact-filled
cornfield (about corn, of course!) using the corn patterns (page 39),
and then place their scarecrows around the field to keep watch.

⭐ SOMETHING TO CROW ABOUT

Invite students to make these boasting crows
to show off their work. First, have them color
and cut out the crow patterns on page 43.
(Provide two wings per child.) Then ask students
to attach a page of their writing or artwork to a
9- by 12-inch sheet of black construction paper and
glue the crow patterns along the edges, as shown.
Display the crows on a cut-paper fence on your
bulletin board to create an attractive harvest scene.

⭐ NATURE'S WONDERS

Create a hands-on, fall table display to provide students with additional
opportunities to explore natural products of the season. Ask students
to collect items that grow or can be found in nature during the fall,
such acorns, leaves, pine cones, gourds, pumpkins, Indian corn, and
nuts. Arrange the items on a table or in a large wicker basket to display
prominently on a table. Then encourage students to pick up, examine, and
talk about the items with others.

★ POP TO IT!

Popcorn is a favorite corn product for kids of all ages! Share the following information with students, then pop a batch of popcorn for them to enjoy. When finished, distribute copies of the popcorn puff stationery (page 44) and have students write what they know about popcorn. Display the pages on a bulletin board, similar to the one shown, for others to read and enjoy. (If desired, use popcorn kernels to fill in the word "POP" on the display.)

HOW DOES POPCORN POP?

Native Americans believed that a small demon lived in each popcorn kernel. When his house was heated to a high temperature, the demon would get so mad he would explode! What really happens is quite simple. Each popcorn kernel contains moisture in its soft center. When the kernel is heated to about 400˚ Fahrenheit, that moisture turns to steam. As the steam expands, if puts pressure on the hard outer shell until the kernel finally "pops" open and the fluffy center turns inside out!

★ POPCORN WORD PLAY

Challenge students to brainstorm as many words as possible that describe popcorn. Encourage them to describe its appearance, taste, smell, sound, and texture. List student responses on chart paper. Afterward, instruct students to use at least ten of the words from the list to write a popcorn-related poem or story. Here are some words you might include on the list:

buttery	oily	sizzle
crispy	pop	warm
crunchy	puffy	white
explosion	salty	yellow

★ POPCORN TALES

Invite students to bind their popcorn-related writing assignments inside the popcorn book cover (page 45). They might write about special events or memories in their life that involved popcorn, imaginary popcorn tales, creative poems or songs, and so on. When finished, invite volunteers to share their writing with classmates.

October Monthly Idea Book © Scholastic Teaching Resources

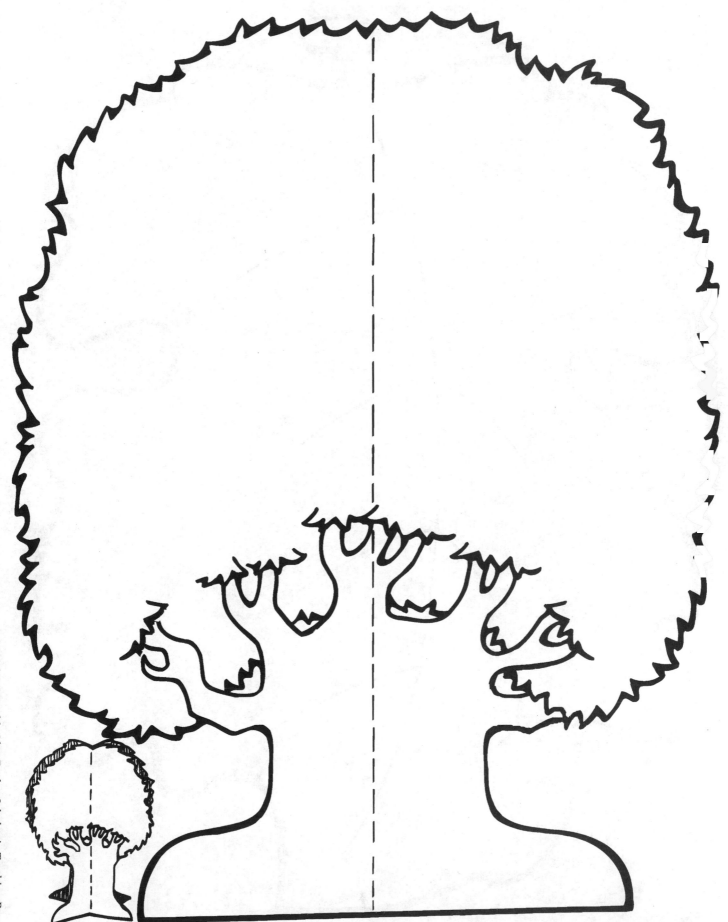

October Monthly Idea Book © Scholastic Teaching Resources

PLACE THIS SIDE ALONG FOLD.

October Monthly Idea Book © Scholastic Teaching Resources

October Monthly Idea Book © Scholastic Teaching Resources

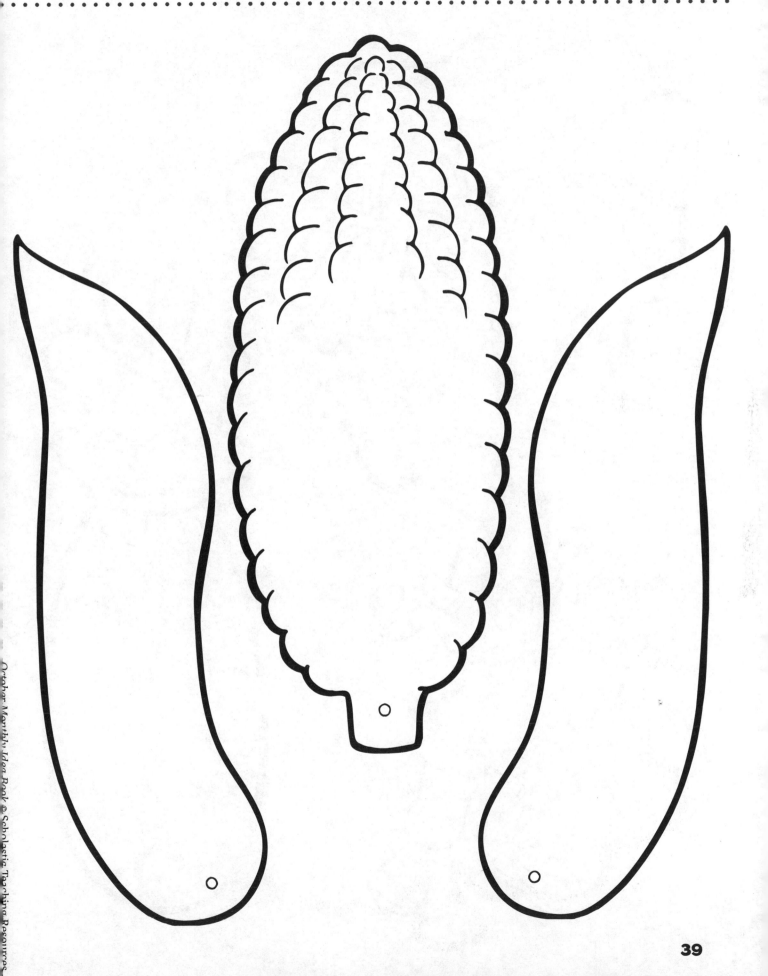

October Monthly Idea Book © Scholastic Teaching Resources

October Monthly Idea Book. © Scholastic Teaching Resources

October Monthly Idea Book © Scholastic Teaching Resources

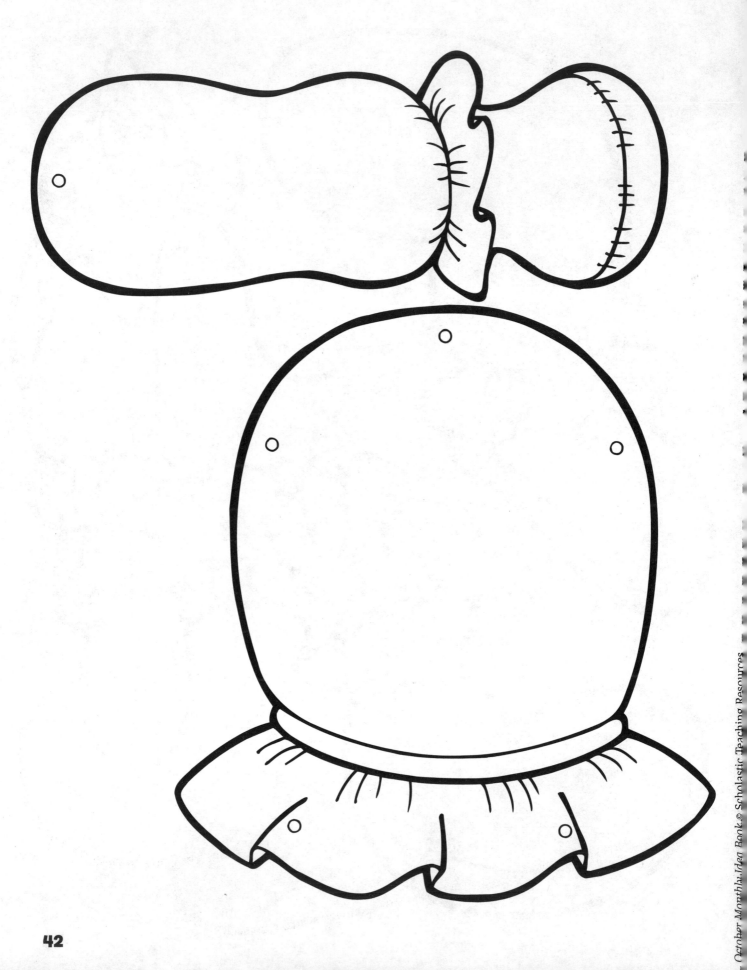

October Monthly Idea Book © Scholastic Teaching Resources

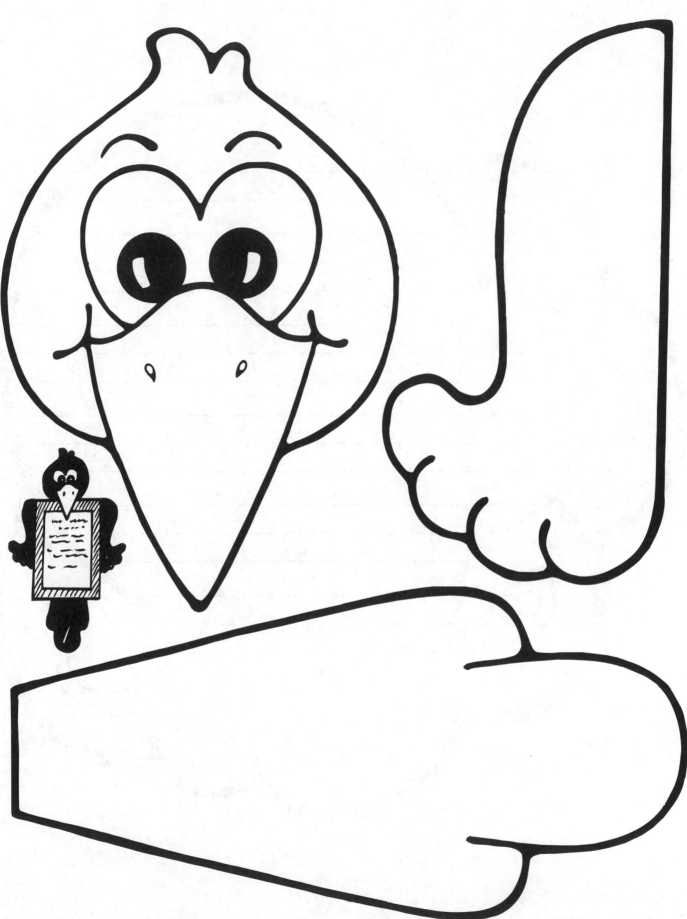

October Monthly Idea Book © Scholastic Teaching Resources

PLACE THIS SIDE ALONG FOLD.

POPCORN

COLUMBUS DAY

On August 3, 1492, Christopher Columbus set sail from Spain in search of a shorter route to the Indies, where he hoped to find gold and spices. He and nearly 90 men sailed west on three ships, the *Niña, Pinta,* and *Santa María,* crossing the uncharted waters of the Atlantic Ocean.

The journey was long and difficult. The crews became terrified at their failure to find land and threatened mutiny. Finally, on October 12, 1492, land was sighted from the *Pinta!* A cannon was fired to signal the discovery. Later that day, the ships made landfall on the island. With the native peoples looking on, Columbus reverently claimed the land for Spain, naming it *San Salvador.* However, he was disappointed not to find the grand civilizations and wealthy cities that had been expected.

Columbus had discovered land that was unknown to Europeans at the time. Although the land was inhabited, it was referred to as the "New World," and King Ferdinand and Queen Isabella of Spain honored Columbus for his discovery. Today, this land is known as the Americas. Throughout our country since the early 1900s, yearly celebrations have been held to commemorate Columbus' historical voyage and discovery. In 1937, President Franklin Roosevelt proclaimed every October 12 as Columbus Day. Since 1971, the holiday has been observed on the second Monday in October.

Suggested Activities

★ COLUMBUS WORD FIND

After sharing about Christopher Columbus, reinforce students' knowledge of related proper names with the word find on page 49. Explain that each word in the puzzle reads across from left to right, or down from top to bottom. Then have students try to find all of the words in the word bank, circling each one as they find it. When finished, you might add the words to a word wall, and encourage students to use them in creative writing assignments like the one suggested at the bottom of the word find.

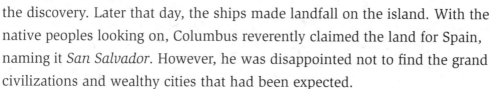

DISCOVER THE AMERICAS

Christopher Columbus' discovery of the Americas changed the history of the world! The land he discovered was unknown to Europeans before Columbus came upon them. Distribute copies of the map (page 50) to students. Review the names of the countries on the map. Then have students find those countries on a world map or globe. Ask them to identify which of the Americas each country is a part of: North America, Central America, or South America. Then encourage students to expand their view of the map to notice how much more land belongs to these three Americas. Remind them that this was all land that Europeans knew nothing about before Columbus' voyage. To wrap up the activity, have students find Spain. Help them tape a length of yarn between that country and San Salvador to show the direction and distance of Columbus' travels.

 ## THREE SHIPS WENT A-SAILING

Instruct small groups to research the voyage of Columbus' three ships, the *Niña, Pinta,* and *Santa María.* Have students in each group create a timeline to mark the significant events of Columbus' travels. Afterward, copy a supply of the three ship patterns (pages 51–52) onto construction paper. Distribute a set of patterns to students and have them color and cut out each one. Then help them fanfold a 12- by 18-inch sheet of blue construction paper (to represent the ocean), cut three slits across the folds—one slit behind the other—and then insert each ship into a slit so that it stands upright in the rippling "water." Finally, encourage students to use their ship props as they share their timelines with the class.

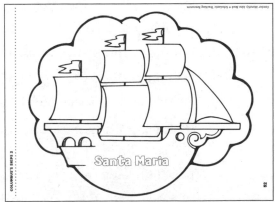

★ JOURNEY JOURNALS

Engage students in creative writing activities. Ask them to choose a situation (below) and write a response or imaginative story about it. Or, invite students to create skits, poems, or songs related to Christopher Columbus and his historic voyage. Encourage them to research their topics to gather factual and interesting information to incorporate into their writing. Students can use the Columbus stationery (page 53) for their final copy.

- You are King Ferdinand or Queen Isabella of Spain, commissioning Christopher Columbus to search for a new route to the Indies.

- You are Columbus preparing to set sail for the Indies.

- You have been chosen to sail on the same ship with Columbus, the *Santa María*.

- You are a native witnessing three ships with strangers landing on your island.

★ PRESENTATION PROPS

Students can create and use props to present their papers, skits, poems, or songs (see Journey Journals) to the class. Or they might use the props to role-play people and events related to Columbus and his voyage. Invite them to choose one of the following props to construct for their presentation:

Sailor Hat: Cut out two hat patterns from black or blue construction paper and one hat emblem pattern from white or yellow paper. (See patterns on page 54.) Glue the emblem to one of the hat cutouts. Then staple the hats together at both ends, fitting the hat to your head.

Columbus Puppet: Color and cut out copies of the puppet patterns (page 55). Glue the cutouts to a paper bag.

Stand-Up Columbus Character: Color and cut out a tagboard copy of the Columbus and spyglass patterns (page 56). Glue the spyglass to Columbus' hand. Then fold back each side of the cutout and stand the character upright on a flat surface.

Columbus Word Find

Find these proper names in the puzzle below:

AMERICA   COLUMBUS   KING FERDINAND   NEW WORLD

NIÑA   PINTA   QUEEN ISABELLA   SAN SALVADOR

SANTA MARIA   SPAIN

```
D V B H Y U J K O L M N H G V B H F R T Y
C O L U M B U S S E R T G Y H U J K I L P
W E R T G Y H P D C V B Q S E R T Y U I P
Z C V F G T H A S W R T U F G H Y U J M N
C F G R T B N I F R T Y E D R Y H J P S Q
S C V B G F D N R T Y H E C O L K I I N G
A M E T Y F E B C D R W N Q X C V T N H U
N E S A N T A M A R I A I F V B G T T D R
S W E T Y G H U I J K Y S D R T Y E A V F
B G T Y U J H F G T V B A M E R I C A T U
W E R T G D V F H F T R B W T Y U P I B N
Q U E F T G H K I N G F E R D I N A N D R
D C V G H B G F V F D S L S R T G Y T R E
D N E W W O R L D F T E L F R T Y G F R E
F B V C D S A N S A L V A D O R F T Y H U
S D F G T Y H U J N B V C X Z D R T G D R
S R V B N M K J G F D N I Ñ A S E F Y H O
```

Which of Columbus' three ships would you have liked to have sailed on?
Explain your answer on the back of this page.

Name of ship: _____

October Monthly Idea Book © Scholastic Teaching Resources

Discover the Americas!

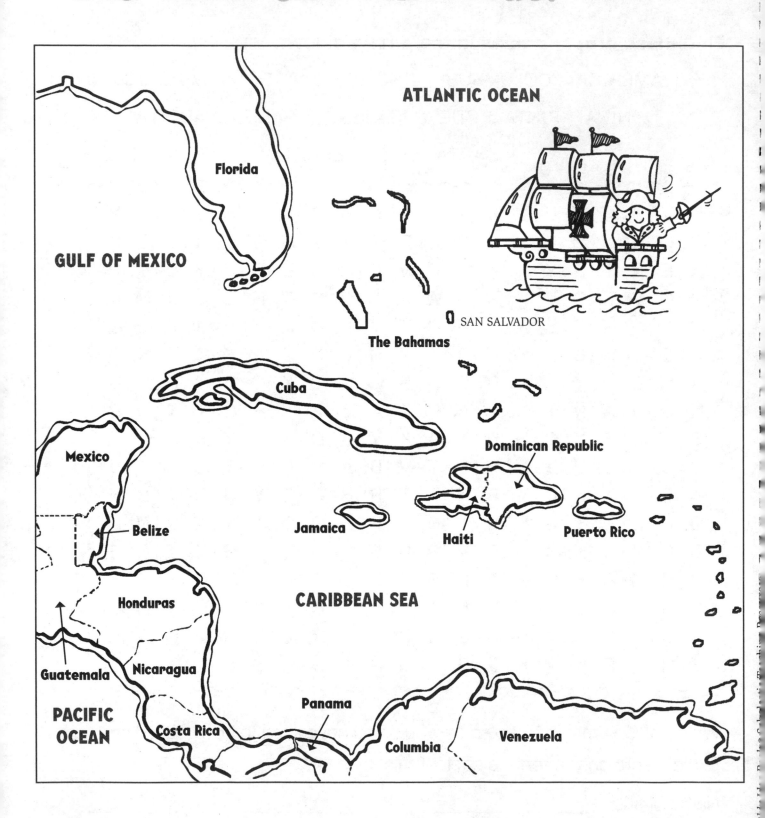

ATLANTIC OCEAN

Florida

GULF OF MEXICO

SAN SALVADOR

The Bahamas

Cuba

Dominican Republic

Mexico

Belize

Jamaica

Haiti

Puerto Rico

CARIBBEAN SEA

Honduras

Guatemala

Nicaragua

PACIFIC OCEAN

Panama

Costa Rica

Columbia

Venezuela

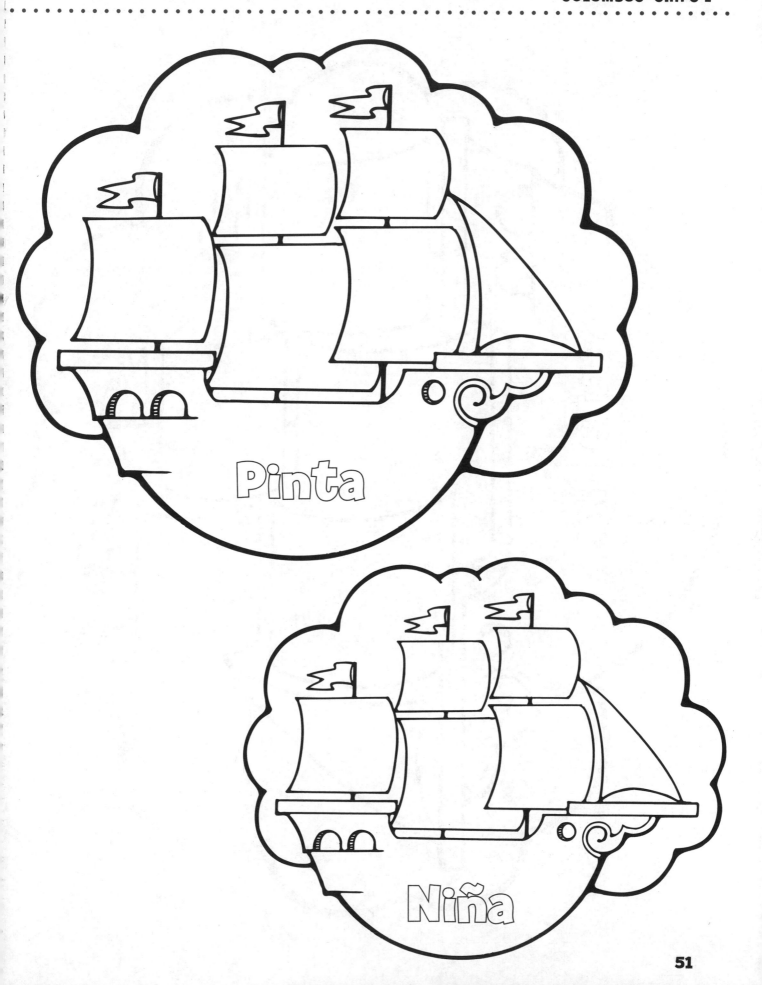

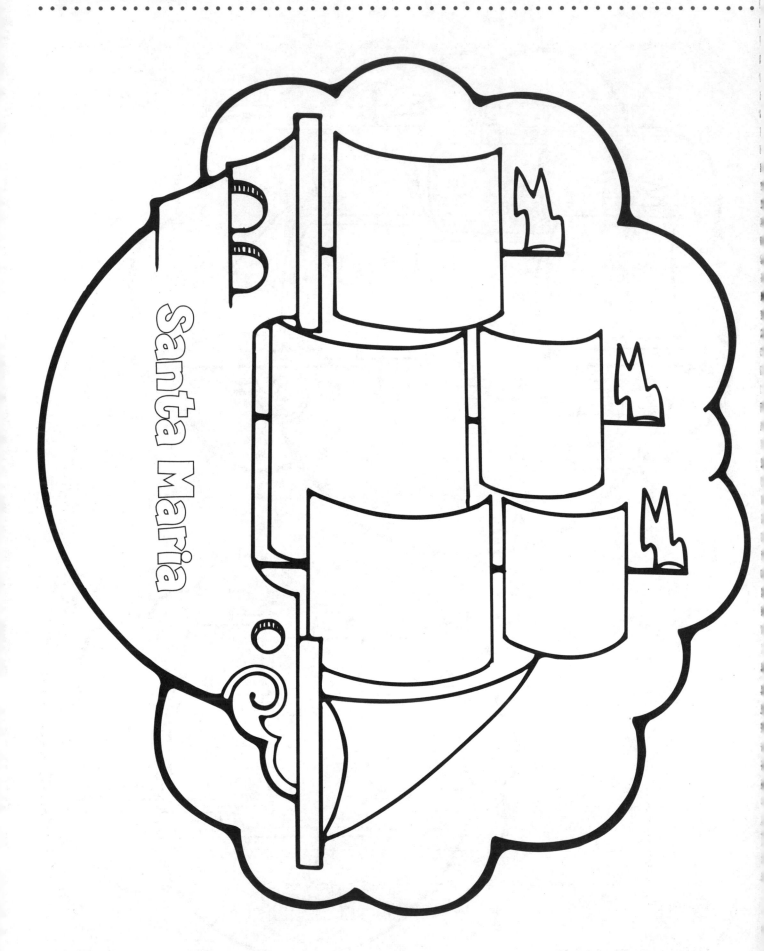

Santa Maria

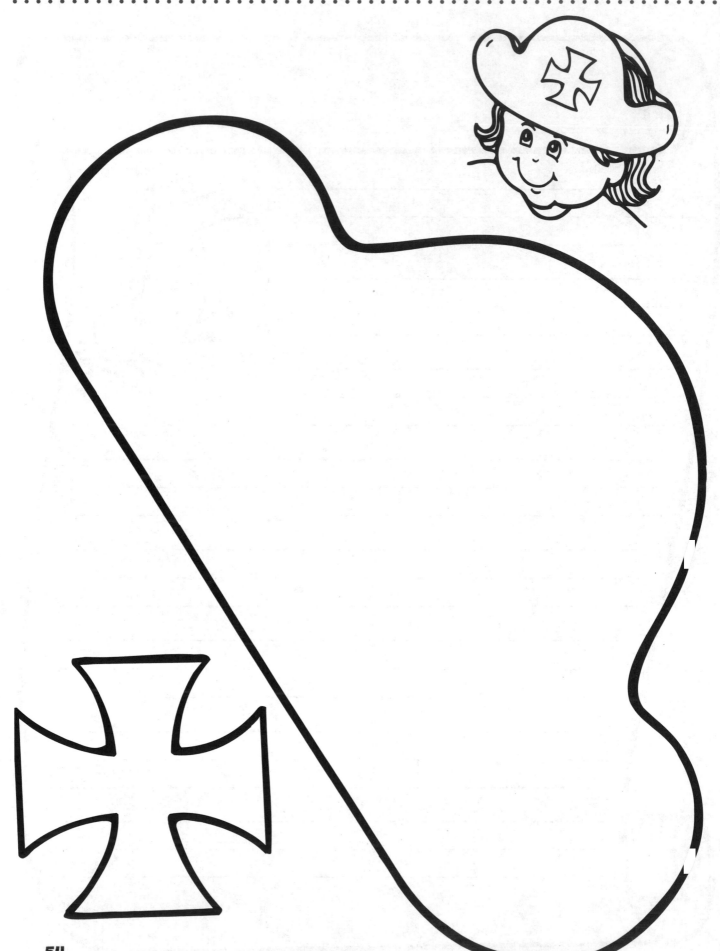

FIRE SAFETY

October is National Fire Prevention Month—a time to emphasize fire safety and prevention practices. Fire is a fascinating element, mesmerizing to watch and comfort-giving in its heat. When used and handled properly, fire offers many benefits, from its use in cooking to providing energy, heat, and light. It can also give pleasure, such as in firework displays or on birthday-cake candles. But fire can also be dangerous, causing damage to property or loss of life. Help students become fire-smart with activities that teach and reinforce critical fire-safety skills.

Suggested Activities

 ## FIRE UP A DISCUSSION

Discuss with students times in which they might see or encounter fire, such as in a fireplace, on birthday candles, at a campfire, or during a fireworks show. Talk about the benefits and the dangers of fire. Then invite students to share what they know about fire safety and ways to prevent unwanted or damaging fires. Write student responses on chart paper. As you continue your studies about fire safety and prevention, invite students to add to or alter the list to elaborate or provide more information.

 ## EMERGENCY!

Do students know what to do if they see a fire, such as a burning building, or another emergency situation? Have them share what they know. Then tell them that first of all, if they are in a burning building, they should get out quickly and stay out. Once safe, they should report the fire to an adult, if possible, so that the adult can call for emergency assistance. If no adult is available, emphasize the importance of dialing 911 (or their local emergency number) to report the situation. Give students practice in dialing and reporting the emergency. You can bring in real phones—landlines or cell phones— with the cords or batteries removed. As they make their imaginary 911 calls, have students practice giving their name and address to the dispatcher (you).

IMPORTANT PHONE NUMBERS

Distribute copies of the form on page 62 to send home with students. Encourage them to ask a parent or other adult in the household to help fill out the phone numbers. Suggest that students post the numbers on a refrigerator, near the phone, or some other conspicuous place where they will be readily available in case of an emergency.

 ## STOP, DROP, AND ROLL

Tell students that if their clothes catch fire, they need to act quickly to extinguish the flames. Explain that fire needs air to keep burning, so it's important to starve the fire of air. To do this, they should not run or jump up and down—this will only create more air for the burning fire. Instead, they should *stop*, *drop* to the ground, and then *roll* back and forth to smother the fire and prevent air from reaching it. Let each child practice these steps by imagining their clothes are on fire. You can also share that if students see another person's clothing on fire, they might try to help by smothering the fire with a blanket, coat, or other large fabric item.

 ## GET OUT!

Review with students what they should do to get out of a burning building as safely as possible. First, ask them to describe what happens to the smoke of a burning fire. Point out that outdoors, smoke rises high into the sky. But in a burning building, it rises to the ceiling and then begins filling in the air space below. Explain that if students are caught in a burning building, and there is smoke, they should drop to their hands and knees, or even their belly, and crawl below the smoke—there, the air will be clearer and allow them to breathe. Also, when trying to escape a burning building, students should feel doors before opening them. If the door is hot, do not open it! A hot door indicates the fire is just on the other side. Have students research and share other safety measures they should follow to get safely out of a burning building. Then invite them to engage in role-playing to practice the safety measures they have learned about.

FAMILY-FIRE ESCAPE PLAN

Ask students to share about their own family's fire-escape plan. Has their family discussed safe ways to get out of their home if it caught fire? Do family members know what to do and where to go once they are out safely? Does each member have a specific responsibility, such as calling 911 or watching over other members? Copy and distribute pages 63–64 to students to take home. Encourage them to discuss the safety measures listed on "In Case of Fire" and to create a fire-escape floorplan with their family. Suggest that they post the pages in their home as reminders and references for fire-safety practices.

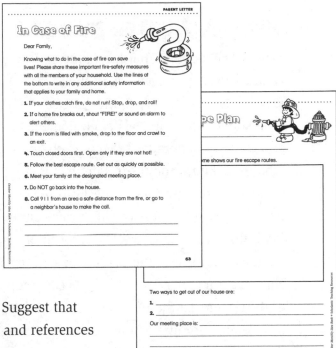

SAFE AND SOUND

How can students make sure their homes are as fire-safe as possible? Invite them to share ways they can help prevent fires at home. List their responses on chart paper. Then pass out copies of the home fire-safety checklist on page 65. Review the items shown, checking off each one that appears on your class list. Discuss things on the checklist that students can do themselves to help make their home safe, and things that an adult should do. Then have students take the checklist home to fill out with their family.

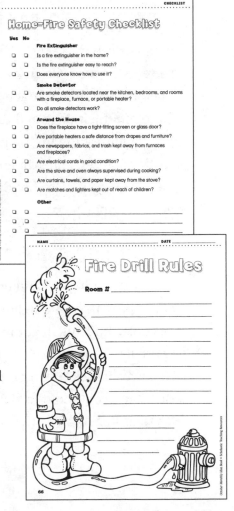

FIRE DRILL

Teach students the school fire drill procedures and your classroom exit plan. You might enlarge a copy of the fire escape route to display, then point out the exit route for the room and building. Afterward, walk students through the exit route several times, checking that they understand where they are to go and wait until signaled to re-enter the building. Emphasize the need for students to move quickly, quietly, and orderly to the designated area. Wrap up by distributing copies of page 66 for students to fill out.

★ OUR FIRE-FIGHTER FRIENDS

Review the clothing that fire fighters wear and the gear they use in their job. If possible, invite a fire fighter to visit the class to talk about his or her equipment and duties. Encourage students to share what they know about fire safety with the fire fighter and to ask questions they have prepared in advance. After the visit, invite students to make fire fighter helmets to wear as a token of what they've learned. To make one, round the corners of a 12- by 18-inch sheet of red construction paper. Help students cut a curved line on the inside of the paper and then fold the cut section up, as shown. Finally, have them cut out a yellow copy of the badge (page 67) to glue to their helmet.

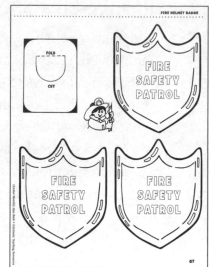

★ FIRE-FIGHTER PAGE FRAMER

Students can make their own fire fighter page holder with the patterns on page 68. Ask them to color and cut out the patterns. Then have students attach the head and feet to the top and bottom of their page and the hands to the sides of the page. You might use the fire fighters to display students' creative writing assignments. Or, enlarge the patterns to make a fire-fighter framer for your class fire drill rules, fire escape map, or general fire safety practices.

★ HOT TOPIC STATIONERY

Liven up writing assignments with stationery ideal for writing about fire safety, fire fighters, or another related topic. For example, students might research fire safety pertaining to a particular holiday, such as Independence Day (fireworks), Halloween (jack-o'-lanterns), or winter holidays (candles). Distribute copies of the stationery on page 69 for students to use for their final drafts.

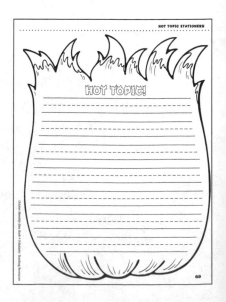

⭐ FIRE-SAFETY BOOK COVER

To add a finishing touch to any writing or research project about fire safety, distribute copies of page 70 for students to use as a book or report cover.

⭐ FIRE-SAFETY BULLETIN BOARD

Create this fire-safety bulletin board to show off what students have learned. First, divide the class into two groups. Ask one group to list the "Do's" of fire prevention, and the other group the "Don'ts." Examples might include "DO check that all smoke detectors are in working order," or "DON'T play with matches!" Once the groups have their lists together, distribute yellow and red copies of the flame stationery on page 69. (You may want to cover the header with "DO" and "DON'T" before copying.) Instruct students to write their fire-prevention words of wisdom on the flames. Then use the flames to create a special fire-prevention bulletin board. You can enlarge the fire-fighter head and hand patterns on page 68 to use as accents on your display.

⭐ FIRE-SAFETY CERTIFICATE

To wrap up your studies on fire safety, present students with a certificate recognizing them for being fire-safe and fire-smart. Copy a supply of the certificates (page 71) and fill out one for each child. Invite students to color their certificates before taking them home to share with their family.

Important Phone Numbers

Emergency   911

Police _____

Fire _____

Ambulance _____

Poison Control _____

Dad's Work _____

Mom's Work _____

Important Phone Numbers

Emergency   911

Police _____

Fire _____

Ambulance _____

Poison Control _____

Dad's Work _____

Mom's Work _____

In Case of Fire

Dear Family,

Knowing what to do in the case of fire can save lives! Please share these important fire-safety measures with all the members of your household. Use the lines at the bottom to write in any additional safety information that applies to your family and home.

1. If your clothes catch fire, do not run! Stop, drop, and roll!

2. If a home fire breaks out, shout "FIRE!" or sound an alarm to alert others.

3. If the room is filled with smoke, drop to the floor and crawl to an exit.

4. Touch closed doors first. Open only if they are not hot!

5. Follow the best escape route. Get out as quickly as possible.

6. Meet your family at the designated meeting place.

7. Do NOT go back into the house.

8. Call 9 I I from an area a safe distance from the fire, or go to a neighbor's house to make the call.

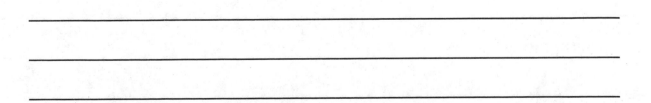

Fire-Escape Plan

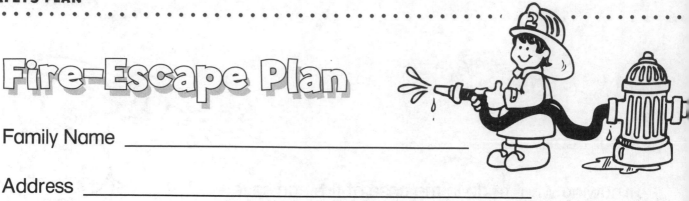

Family Name _____

Address _____

This floor plan of our home shows our fire escape routes.

[ ]

Two ways to get out of our house are:

1. _____

2. _____

Our meeting place is: _____

_____

Home-Fire Safety Checklist

Yes   No

Fire Extinguisher

❑   ❑   Is a fire extinguisher in the home?

❑   ❑   Is the fire extinguisher easy to reach?

❑   ❑   Does everyone know how to use it?

Smoke Detector

❑   ❑   Are smoke detectors located near the kitchen, bedrooms, and rooms with a fireplace, furnace, or portable heater?

❑   ❑   Do all smoke detectors work?

Around the House

❑   ❑   Does the fireplace have a tight-fitting screen or glass door?

❑   ❑   Are portable heaters a safe distance from drapes and furniture?

❑   ❑   Are newspapers, fabrics, and trash kept away from furnaces and fireplaces?

❑   ❑   Are electrical cords in good condition?

❑   ❑   Are the stove and oven always supervised during cooking?

❑   ❑   Are curtains, towels, and paper kept away from the stove?

❑   ❑   Are matches and lighters kept out of reach of children?

Other

❑   ❑   _____

❑   ❑   _____

❑   ❑   _____

Fire Drill Rules

Room # _____

_____

_____

_____

_____

_____

_____

_____

_____

_____

FOLD

CUT

FIRE
SAFETY
PATROL

FIRE
SAFETY
PATROL

FIRE
SAFETY
PATROL

October Monthly Idea Book © Scholastic Teaching Resources

FIRE DEPT.

7

October Monthly Idea Book © Scholastic Teaching Resources

HOT TOPIC!

PLACE THIS SIDE ALONG FOLD.

FIRE SAFETY

Name

October Monthly Idea Book © Scholastic Teaching Resources

Fire-Safety Certificate

Congratulations to

_____

Student

You are a fire-safe and fire-smart kid!

_____

Teacher

_____

Date

Fire-Safety Certificate

Congratulations to

_____

Student

You are a fire-safe and fire-smart kid!

_____

Teacher

_____

Date

October Monthly Idea Book © Scholastic Teaching Resources

DINOSAURS

Dinosaurs ruled the earth for nearly 100 million years. Since the identification of the first dinosaur fossil in 1822, scientists have learned a great deal about these fascinating creatures. The word *dinosaur* means "terrible lizard," although these creatures were not actually lizards, but belonged to a special group of reptiles. Some dinosaurs walked on two feet, while others walked on all four. Some were strictly plant-eaters and others fierce meat-eaters. Some dinosaurs preferred living in or near water, while others thrived in drier climates.

Scientists are still puzzled over why the dinosaurs disappeared. Many believe that an impact event, such as a comet or asteroid crashing into the earth, led to the extinction of dinosaurs. There is also evidence that change in climate played a role in their extinction. Although these prehistoric creatures no longer walk the Earth, their remains tell us a lot about their size, their lifestyles, and where they lived.

Suggested Activities

 ### FINDING FOSSILS

Tell students that paleontologists are scientists who search for and study fossils. Most of what we know about dinosaurs is due to the work of paleontologists. These experts explore, examine, measure, and compare fossils of prehistoric creatures and other life forms to gather information about the size and build of dinosaurs, what they ate, how they moved about, and where they lived. To find out more, students can search Internet sites, library books, and other sources to learn about how one becomes a paleontologist, the tools they use in their work, and where they might find fossils to study. Invite students to share their findings with the class.

 ### MAKE A FOSSIL

Explain that fossils are formed when part of an animal or plant leaves an impression in soil that hardens into rock over a long period of time. To help students understand how fossils are formed, invite them to make their own fossils. First, mix enough water with classroom clay to make "clay slip" (a paste-like clay that can be easily spread). Then help students fill the bottom of a plastic container, such as a butter or cottage cheese tub, with a layer of the clay slip, about one inch deep. Have them smooth the surface with a spatula, gently press an object into it, and then remove the object, leaving an impression in the clay. Students might make impressions of objects such as leaves, twigs, or nuts. Allow the clay to dry for two to three days.

After students examine and share their hardened fossils with classmates, tell them that paleontologists often make casts of fossils. Have them do the same with this simple idea. Spray each impression with a non-stick cooking spray. Then spread a thick layer of fresh plaster of Paris over the imprint. When the plaster dries, students can lift the cast carefully from its mold.

★ DINOSAUR PICTURE PROPS

Use the dinosaur patterns on pages 77–80 in a variety of ways to help students learn about dinosaurs. For example, you can enlarge the patterns for use on bulletin board displays. Or have students research to find the name and facts about each kind of dinosaur. Ask them to write their facts on note cards (one fact per card), then post the cards next to the corresponding dinosaurs. You might also post word cards featuring dinosaur-related vocabulary on the patterns.

★ DINOSAUR MATCH

Copy and cut out the dinosaur bones on pages 80–82. Review the text on each bone and invite students to share what they know about that dinosaur. To make a matching game, copy the dinosaur patterns (pages 77–80). Then have students match each bone to the dinosaur it describes.

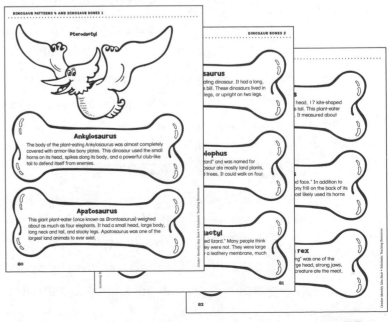

73

BONE UP ON DINOSAURS

Use an enlarged bone pattern from page 80 to create a tagboard template. Then trace and cut out a supply of large bones (from white construction paper or bulletin board paper) to label with dinosaur names. Display the bones on a bulletin board. Then ask students to choose a dinosaur to research. Have them write dinosaur facts on cards to post under the bone for their selected dinosaur. If desired, invite students to add drawings of their dinosaur, too.

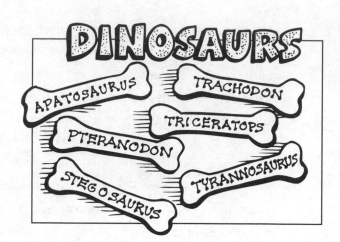

DINOSAUR DISCOVERIES

As students make their discoveries about different kinds of dinosaurs, encourage them to organize and compile the information into a nonfiction book about these creatures. To liven up their work, invite them to cut out and color the pattern on page 83 to use as their book cover. Following are a few topics they might include in their book:

- factual information about different dinosaurs

- comparison of meat-eaters vs. plant-eaters (including sizes and survival tactics)

- climate and environmental conditions that helped dinosaurs thrive

- the cause of dinosaur extinction (include at least two theories generally believed by scientists)

- where dinosaur bones have been found (also include areas in which few to no dinosaur fossils have been found)

PREHISTORIC STATIONERY

As students prepare to write their final copy of research reports, or other nonfiction text about dinosaurs, distribute copies of the stationery (page 84) for their use. Students can also use the stationery for poems, songs, acrostics, and other creative writing assignments related to dinosaurs.

UP-TO-DATE ABOUT DINOSAURS

It was once believed that all dinosaurs were cold-blooded creatures that traveled and moved at a slow pace. Today, however, many scientists believe that several warm-blooded dinosaurs existed, and there were some that could run very fast. Also, until recently, many believed that dinosaurs paid little attention to their young. Now, discoveries have revealed that some dinosaurs were actually attentive parents that cared for and protected their young, similar to how many birds care for their chicks. In fact, some dinosaurs lived together in colonies. After sharing this information, ask students to do research to learn more about how scientists' beliefs and theories have changed or evolved as more has been learned about different kinds of dinosaurs. Invite them to share about the new information and discoveries that have occurred over time. Encourage students to also tell about how scientists come to make new conclusions about these prehistoric reptiles.

 ## HOW BIG IS A DINOSAUR?

Children—and adults, for that matter—have a hard time imagining large numbers and sizes. Help students better understand the sizes of different dinosaurs with this activity. First, have them choose two or three dinosaurs to research. Ask them to find and jot down information about the estimated height and length of each dinosaur. Then take the class outdoors to the playground or other open space. Bring along a long measuring tape, the dinosaur measurements, and two rolls of masking tape (each a different color). Have students measure and mark off each dinosaur's dimensions on the ground, using one color of masking tape for height and another for length. Finally, invite students to lie down next to each line of tape to compare their own height to that of each dinosaur. If desired, ask students to lay head to foot to see how many times more (in length or height) the dinosaur is to the average student. Before doing this exercise, you might have students make estimates to compare to their actual results.

★ PET DINOSAURS

Which students in your class have pets? After students
share about their pets, ask whether they would like to have
a pet dinosaur, if the creatures still lived today. If so, what
kind would they want? Discuss their responses and the pros
and cons of having this kind of pet. Then invite students to
imagine they do have a pet dinosaur. Have them research
that dinosaur to learn about its size, weight, food and
environmental needs, and other characteristics. Have them
write an imaginary story about their pet dinosaur. Encourage them to carefully
consider the various problems they might encounter by owning such an unusual
pet. For example: *Where would it sleep? What would it eat? How would they
get food for it? How would their neighbors react? How would the other family pets
relate to it?* Tell students that although their stories can be fun and entertaining,
they must present actual facts about each dinosaur, as well.

★ DINOSAUR HELPERS

Keep track of your classroom helpers with this "fun-osaurus" idea. Use the
dinosaur patterns (pages 77–80) to create display pieces for a helper board.
Label each dinosaur with a classroom job, adding the ending "-osaurus"
to it. Your labels might include "Messengerosaurus," "Eraserosaurus,"
"Leaderosaurus," "Petosaurus," and so on. Then cut out colorful paper dinosaur
eggs to label with student names. To assign a job, simply display the student's
egg with the dinosaur labeled with his or her job.

★ REWARD-OSAURS!

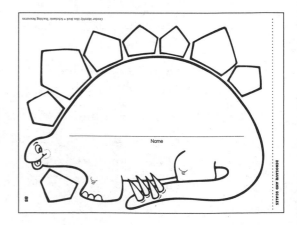

To create a reward board, ask students to cut out
colored copies of the dinosaur and scales patterns
(page 85), and write their name on the dinosaur.
Place all of the scales in a basket near the display.
Then, as students meet a pre-established goal, such as
completing an assignment, invite them to add a scale
to their dinosaur. After they collect a given number
of scales, present students with a special reward.
Alternately, you might use the display for grouping.
Simply label the dinosaurs with group names. To assign groups, place
scales labeled with students' names on the dinosaurs for their groups.

Tyrannosaurus rex

Triceratops

Ankylosaurus

Parasaurolophus

Edmontosaurus

October Monthly Idea Book © Scholastic Teaching Resources

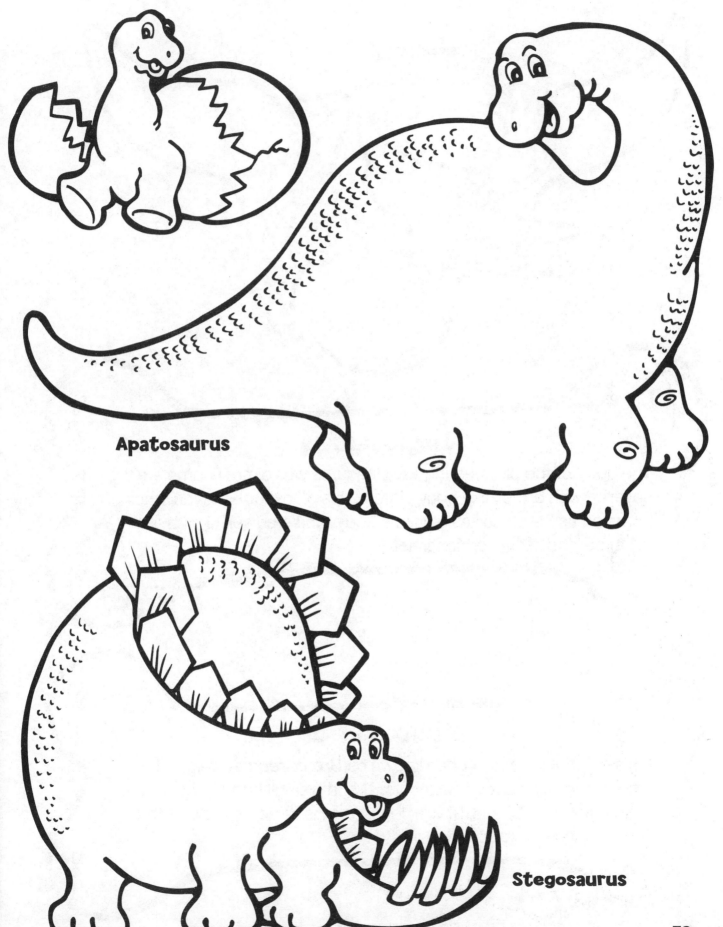

Apatosaurus

Stegosaurus

October Monthly Idea Book ©Scholastic Teaching Resources

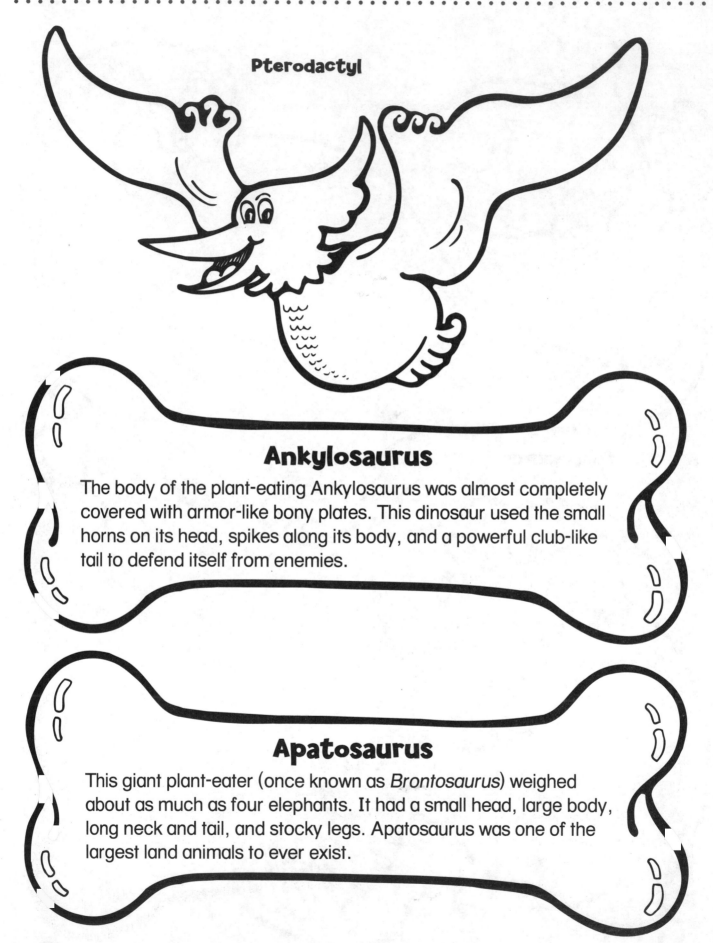

Pterodactyl

Ankylosaurus

The body of the plant-eating Ankylosaurus was almost completely covered with armor-like bony plates. This dinosaur used the small horns on its head, spikes along its body, and a powerful club-like tail to defend itself from enemies.

Apatosaurus

This giant plant-eater (once known as *Brontosaurus*) weighed about as much as four elephants. It had a small head, large body, long neck and tail, and stocky legs. Apatosaurus was one of the largest land animals to ever exist.

Edmontosaurus

Edmontosaurus was a large plant-eating dinosaur. It had a long, wide mouth that resembled a duck's bill. These dinosaurs lived in large groups and walked on all four legs, or upright on two legs.

Parasaurolophus

Parasaurolophus means "crested lizard" and was named for the large crest on its head. This dinosaur ate mostly land plants, getting its food from the ground and trees. It could walk on four legs, or upright on two legs.

Pterodactyl

The name *Pterodactyl* means "winged lizard." Many people think pterodactyls were dinosaurs, but they were not. They were large flying reptiles with wings covered by a leathery membrane, much like the wings of a bat.

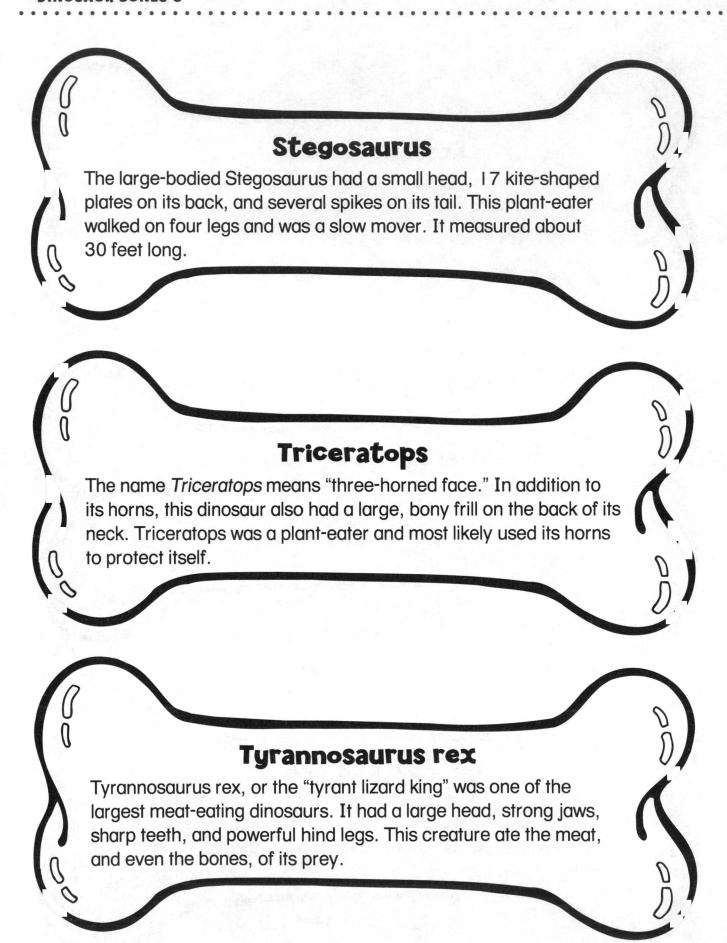

Stegosaurus

The large-bodied Stegosaurus had a small head, 17 kite-shaped plates on its back, and several spikes on its tail. This plant-eater walked on four legs and was a slow mover. It measured about 30 feet long.

Triceratops

The name *Triceratops* means "three-horned face." In addition to its horns, this dinosaur also had a large, bony frill on the back of its neck. Triceratops was a plant-eater and most likely used its horns to protect itself.

Tyrannosaurus rex

Tyrannosaurus rex, or the "tyrant lizard king" was one of the largest meat-eating dinosaurs. It had a large head, strong jaws, sharp teeth, and powerful hind legs. This creature ate the meat, and even the bones, of its prey.

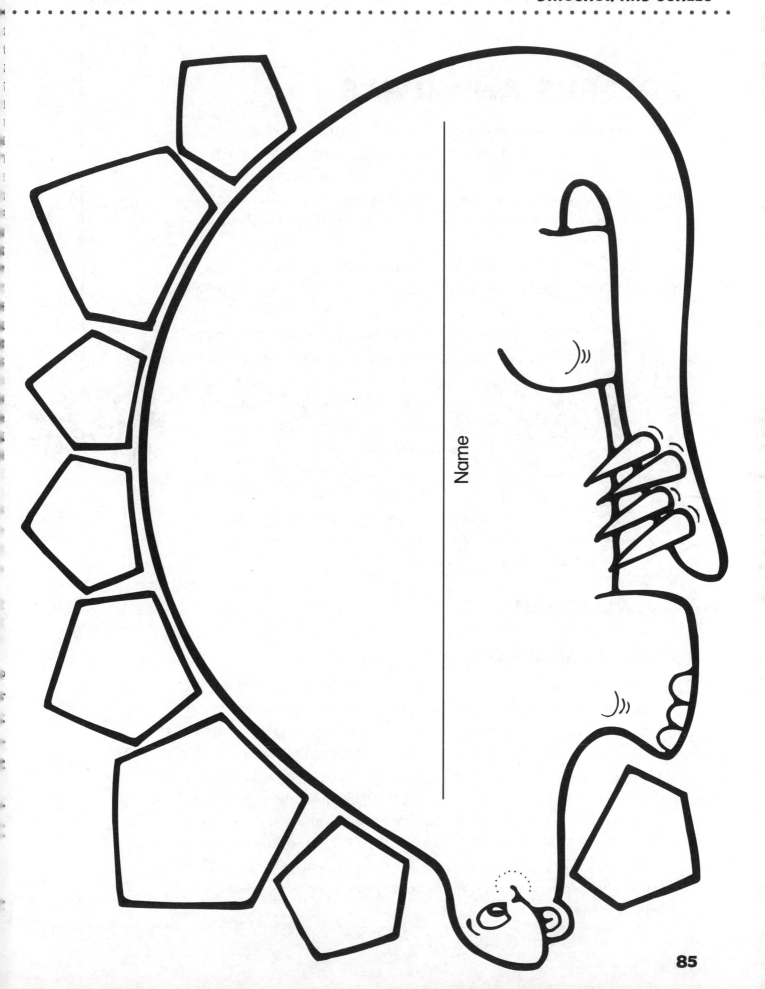

Name

SPIDERS AND OWLS

Spiders can be found just about everywhere. In fact, studies have shown that you're almost always within ten feet of a spider. But the more than 30,000 species of these eight-legged creatures are not insects—they are arachnids! With their spinnerets, fangs, and somewhat intimidating appearance, students will be glad to know that most spiders are harmless to humans (although a few are poisonous).

Spiders spinning their webs overnight might encounter trouble if an owl is nearby. Most owls spend their nights in search of prey—and spiders are often on the menu! Features that make owls uniquely suited for nocturnal activity include keen eyesight, excellent hearing, sharp talons for catching prey, and feathers specially adapted for silent flight. Like spiders, these birds can be found in many places, such as forests, jungles, swamps, deserts, caves, the Arctic tundra, and even in your back yard.

Pique students' interest with this fascinating information about spiders and owls, then entice them to speculate and learn more about these wonderful creatures with the following activities.

Suggested Activities

★ OBSERVING SPIDERS

Gently capture a nonpoisonous spider in a large, clear jar to bring in for students to observe. To create the jar habitat, place some long twigs in the jar and add a few drops of water to the bottom. After capturing the spider, cover the jar with cotton gauze and secure with a rubber band. (For the spider's food, slip a fly or other insect into the jar.) In class, provide students with magnifying glasses so they can examine the spider more thoroughly through the clear jar. Encourage them to share their observations about how the spider looks, how or what it eats, and its activity. List their observations on chart paper to use later for discussion points as students research and learn more about spiders. When students finish their observations, release the spider safely outdoors.

★ THE SPIN ON SPIDERS

Tell students that more than 3,000 varieties of spiders inhabit the United States. Most of these spiders are harmless, however a few can be harmful to humans. Share the following information, then encourage students to choose one of these or any other spider of their choice to research and learn more about. As they search the Internet, nonfiction library books, and other resources, have students look for information such as the spider's physical characteristics, where it lives, how it spins its web, its food preferences, and how it cares for its young. To help students gather and organize their findings, distribute copies of page 94 to get them started.

Black Widow: This spider is the most poisonous spider in the United States—but only the female, which is recognized by her shiny black or brown color and the red, hourglass shape on her body. Black widows build webs from very strong silk. They eat flies, grasshoppers, moths, and even other spiders.

Brown Recluse: This poisonous spider likes to live alone and be let alone, but its venom can be very harmful to humans. Unlike most spiders, it has six eyes rather than eight. It also has a dark brown violin shape on its back. The recluse usually hides and builds its web in dark and secluded areas.

★ SPIDER-WEB BINGO

Reinforce spider-related vocabulary with the spider web game board on page 95. Distribute the Bingo boards and ask students to write a word that names, describes, or relates to spiders in each section of the web. You might work with them first to create a list of words that they can refer to when filling out their webs. To make caller cards, write each word on a separate card and place in a paper bag. Then invite a caller to draw one card at a time from the bag and read the word aloud. Ask players to cover that word if it appears on their web. (Provide a good supply of game markers; dried beans work well.) The first player to cover all of his or her words, calls out "Bingo!" If that player covered all of the correct words, he or she wins the game.

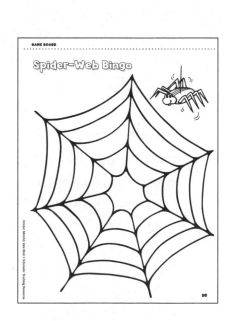

★ CATCH A SPIDER WEB

Here's a clever way to catch a real spider web to display for students to examine! First, find a web (absent the spider) and lay newspaper on the ground under the web. Spray both sides of the web with a light layer of black spray paint. While the paint is still wet, bend a sheet of white paper and touch it gently to the center of the web (the wet web will stick to the paper). Slowly straighten the paper to "capture" the rest of the web. Then carefully pull the web away from its anchors and set it aside to allow the paint to dry. As students study the web, encourage them to note the pattern, how the silk connects to form the web, and any other interesting features about the web.

★ STUDENT-MADE SPIDER WEB

Place a large circle of bulletin board paper in the center of the floor and have students sit around it. Give one child a large ball of yarn (in a contrasting color to the paper) and have the child tape the end of the yarn to the edge of the paper. Ask the student to name a spider fact and then pass the yarn to a child on the opposite side of the circle. This child tapes the yarn in place, states a fact, and passes the yarn to a child opposite him or her. Have students repeat the process, weaving the yarn back and forth to create a web. Continue until each child has had a turn. When finished attach the yarn web to a bulletin board. Finally, invite students to attach spider fact cards around the web and create their own spiders to attach to the web. (They might make the 3-D spider or egg-carton spider, as described below and on page 89, for this purpose.)

★ SPIDER CRAFTS

Invite students to make their own spiders with these simple ideas. Copy the spider patterns (pages 96 and 97) onto dark paper. Distribute the copies to students according to the type of spider they want to make: a 3-D spider or an egg-carton spider. For the 3-D spider, students simply accordion-fold the legs along the lines and then stand their spider upright on a flat surface. For the egg-carton spider, students fold the legs along the line, then glue an egg-cup body to the center of the spider. For either spider, students can use paint and other craft materials to add patterns and embellishments.

★ LEGGY SPIDER

Suspend these cute spiders in your classroom to show off students' spider knowledge. Distribute copies of the pattern on page 98 for students to cut out. Ask them to write facts or other interesting information about a particular spider, or spiders in general, on the body of their spider cutout. For legs, have students cut eight long strips of construction paper, fanfold the strips, and attach them to the spider body. Finally, fold up the head and add yarn to hang the spider from the ceiling, a clothesline, or windows.

★ SNOWFLAKE WEBS

Discuss how spiders spin their silk and the different ways they use it. Also talk about the types of webs that spiders weave. Then invite students to create these unique snowflake webs, as directed:

1. Fold a square of white paper in half and then again in thirds. Trim to create the shape, as shown.

2. With the paper folded to create a triangle, cut away narrow sections as shown, alternating cuts from one folded edge to the next.

3. Unfold the paper carefully to reveal the spider web.

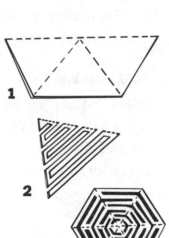

★ SPIDER-AND-WEB MATCH

Copy a supply of the spider and web patterns on page 99. Cut out and use the patterns for learning center activities. For example, you might write a math fact on each spider and the answer on a web. (To make the activity self-checking, write the correct answer on the back of the spider.) You can also use the patterns for matching words that belong to the same word family, matching words and their meanings, or matching synonym or homophone pairs.

★ SPIDER GAMES

Spider and Fly: This simple outdoor game will delight your students. First, choose one student to be Spider and another to be Fly. Ask the other students to stand in a circle and hold hands to create a human "web." To play, have Fly stand inside the circular web and Spider stand on the outside. Have the students forming the web circle around clockwise until you give a signal, such as clapping your hands. On this signal, students stop circling and Spider tries to dart inside the web to tag Fly. At the same time, Fly might dart out of the web to avoid being tagged. Students who are part of the web can help Fly escape by raising or lowering their arms to block Spider. After a given number of attempts, if Spider fails to tag Fly, call the game a draw. Then play again, inviting different students to take the role of Spider and Fly.

Spider Relay: Get students moving with these spider-related tag-team relays. First, divide the class into several small teams. Set up a start and finish line for each relay. Explain that each child on a team will perform the action for that relay as they make their way to the finish line and back to tag the next team member. When finished, announce the winning team for that relay. At the end of all of the relays, offer students a refreshing spider-related snack.

> **Spider Walk**—From a sitting position, have students lean back and place both hands on the floor. Have them lift their body weight and walk forward on all fours.

> **Fly Flurry**—Have students stand on their knees and then flap their arms as they knee-walk to the finish line and back.

> **Spider Egg Carry**—Give students a volleyball to balance on the palm of one hand as they quickly walk forward. For a greater challenge, have students walk backward as they balance the ball.

⭐ WISE ABOUT OWLS

Owls have features that make them fairly easy to distinguish from other types of birds. Share the facts about owls (below) with students. Then invite students to choose, research, and write about one type of owl such as the Barn Owl, Burrowing Owl, Elf Owl, Great Horned Owl, Screech Owl, or Snowy Owl.

- Most owls are nocturnal—they are active at night.

- Owls have large, round heads and flat facial disks.

- Owls have large eyes and keen eyesight. They see very well in the dark.

- Owls can only look forward, but they can turn their heads to look directly behind them.

- Owls have excellent hearing. Some owls have ear tufts—feathers that look like ears.

- The soft edges of an owl's feathers allow it to fly silently.

- Owls are birds of prey, or raptors. They hunt, kill, and eat other animals.

- An owl uses its talons (sharp claws) to catch its prey.

⭐ OWL PAGE FRAMER

To display students' owl research papers, give them the owl page-framer patterns (page 100) to color and cut out. (Provide two wings per child.) Have them mount their page on a 9- by 12-inch sheet of brown or orange construction paper. Then have them glue the owl patterns to the edges of the paper, as shown.

⭐ OWL BOOK COVER

As students research, gather, and write information about owls, encourage them to organize their materials and compile them into a book. They can use the book cover (page 101) to bind their pages together. When completed, invite students to share their books with classmates.

STAND-UP OWL

These stand-up owls make nice display pieces to call attention to owl facts and other interesting information that students want to share about these nocturnal birds. Distribute 9- by 12-inch sheets of orange or yellow construction paper and copies of the patterns (page 102) to students. (Copy two wings for each child.) Then have students follow these directions to make the stand-up owl:

1. Write information about your owl on the center of the construction paper.

2. To make the owl's body, tape or glue the ends of your paper together to form a tube.

3. Color and cut out the owl patterns. Glue the head to the top of the body.

4. Fold the beak in half at the center. Then fold back each flap and glue in place under the eyes.

5. Fold back the flaps on the wings and glue to the sides of the body.

6. Fold up the flap on the feet and glue to the inside of the body tube.

OWL MASK

Students can wear this owl mask as a prop when sharing owl-related facts, poems, or songs with the class or to act out owl-related skits. To make, copy the mask pattern (page 103) onto tagboard. Have students color and cut out their mask. Then help them cut out the eyeholes and attach string to both sides.

WISE-OWL MATH

Reinforce math facts with this fun game. Ask six students to sit in the center of a circle formed by the other students. Select one student to be Wise Owl. Ask Wise Owl to "fly" around the outside of the circle, "land" behind a seated student, and tap that student on the shoulder. Wise Owl then calls out a math fact, such as "nine times three." If the student knows the answer, he or she answers it. If not, the student can choose a child in the middle of the circle to give the answer. When a child answers correctly, that child switches places with Wise Owl and the game continues. Play until every student has had a chance to be Wise Owl and to answer a math fact.

★ GIVE A HOOT!

Explain that the phrase "to give a hoot" simply means to care about something. Do students "give a hoot" about anything in particular? Invite them to tell about some of the things they care about. Their responses might include individual concerns or more universal problems, such as world hunger or war. Make a list of students' concerns on the chalkboard. Then ask them to choose an item from the list and write a short essay telling why they "give a hoot" about that issue. Later, encourage students to share their essay with the class. Wrap up the activity by telling them that "caring" can be extended into action, such as by contributing to a charity, helping clean up the environment, or writing to a school principal or even to a congressman about their concern.

★ WISE ADVICE

The ancient Greeks believed that owls represent wisdom and knowledge. Their large eyes make the birds look especially wise. Although owls are no more intelligent than many other birds, use the owl as a mascot to answer queries for advice from your students. To make the advice box, cover an empty tissue box with colorful paper. Write "Dear Wise Owl" on the box and add a paper owl cutout. Then explain that when students have a problem or important question, they can jot it down and put it in the box. Their situations can be real or imaginary, and they do not need to sign their names. To use, check the box throughout the week, periodically removing entries to read aloud to the class. Then brainstorm with students ways to respond to or solve the question or problem.

★ WHO-O-O-O AM I?

Use this bulletin board to introduce students to historical or important people and places. First, top the board with an owl character cutout. Then choose several places or people to feature on the display. Cut out pictures of the subjects from magazines, newspapers, or other sources. Mount the pictures on the bulletin board along with a few clues about each one. Then challenge students to use their research skills to identify the mystery pictures.

My Spider Report

_____

Spider Name

This is a picture of my spider and its web.

This spider is . . .   ❑ poisonous   ❑ nonpoisonous

This spider can be found _____.

It eats _____.

This spider has . . . [   ] legs and [   ] eyes.

Some interesting facts about this spider:

_____

_____

Spider-Web Bingo

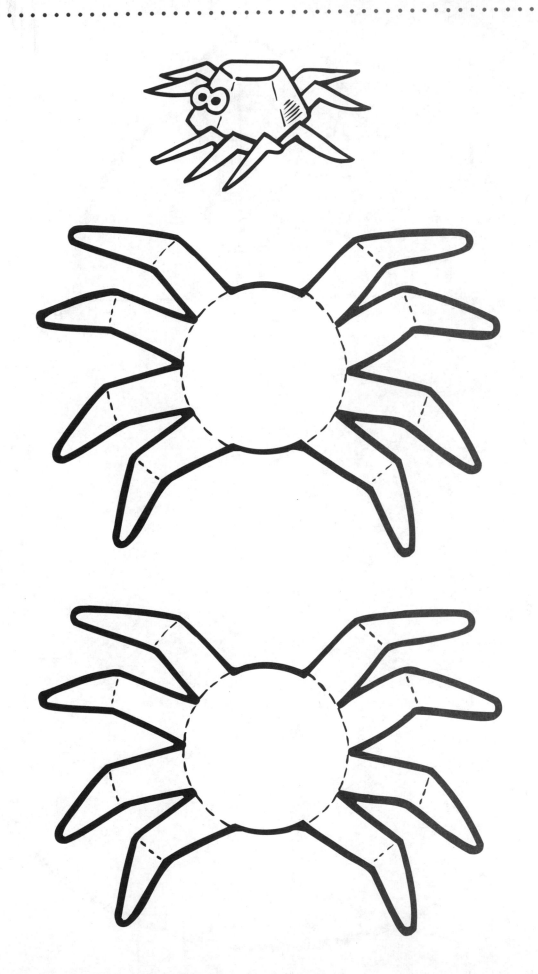

October Monthly Idea Book © Scholastic Teaching Resources

October Monthly Idea Book © Scholastic Teaching Resources

PLACE THIS SIDE ALONG FOLD.

October Monthly Idea Book © Scholastic Teaching Resources

October Monthly Idea Book © Scholastic Teaching Resources

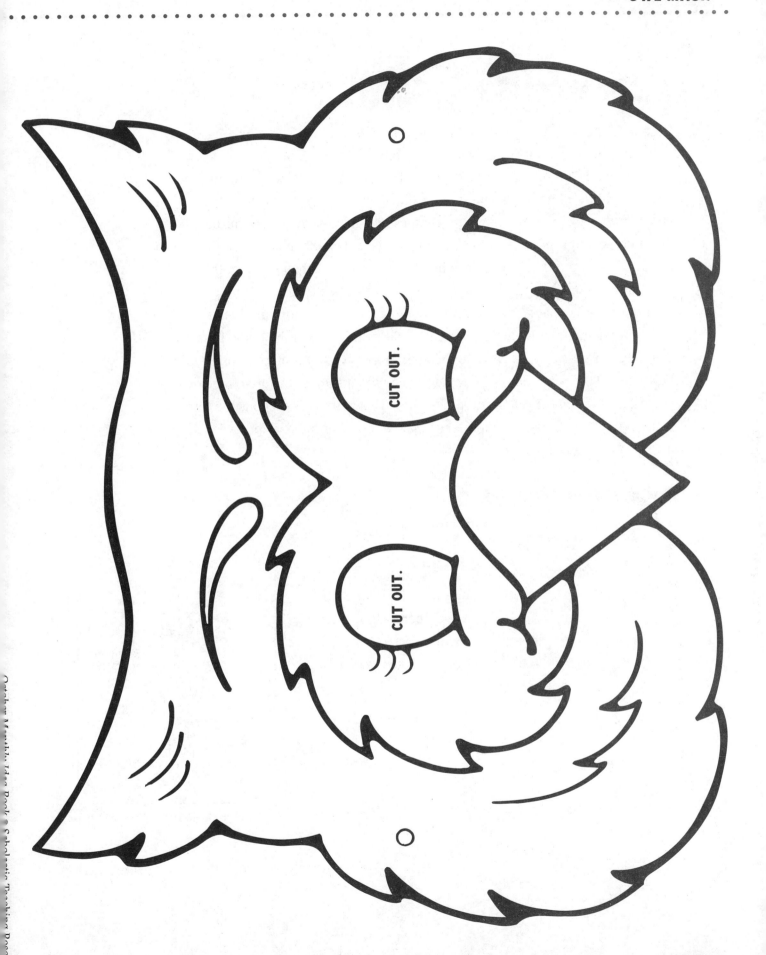

CUT OUT.

CUT OUT.

October Monthly Idea Book © Scholastic Teaching Resources

SKELETONS

No bones about it! With Halloween just around the corner, students are sure to have an interest in learning about skeletons.

Our bodies are made up of 206 skeletal bones. Without skeletons, our body would be a shapeless mass, much like a jellyfish. While most of our bones provide support and strength, some serve another important purpose—they encase and protect sensitive and vital organs. For example, the skull surrounds and protects the brain. The rib cage and breastbone protect the lungs and heart.

Bones are as alive as we are. Although they may seem stiff and lifeless, our bones actually grow and replace cells like other parts of the body. In fact, over a seven-year period, each bone in our body is slowly replaced until it is a new bone! The inside of our bones are filled with a spongy material. *Marrow* is produced in the center of our large bones. This marrow is responsible for making the red and white bloods cells that we need for life and to have a healthy immune system.

Suggested Activities

 ## HELLO, BONES!

To introduce students to the different bones in our skeleton, display a copy of page 107. Point out each bone, name it, and tell its common name. If desired, distribute copies to students for use with other activities in this unit. Afterward, students can take the diagrams home to share with their family.

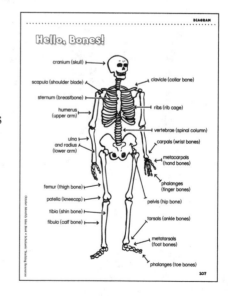

★ SKELETON MATCH

After students are familiar with the scientific and common names of different bones in their body, have them complete the matching activities on page 108. Then give their skeleton knowledge a workout with a game of "Mr. Skeleton says...," in which students touch the bone that's named to complete a sentence, such as "Mr. Skeleton says . . . touch your *cranium*." (This game is an adaptation of "Simon Says.")

★ MR. SKELETON

Enlarge the Mr. Skeleton patterns (pages 109–113) on poster board. Cut out the pieces and assemble the skeleton with brass fasteners. Then display "Mr. Skeleton" in a prominent area of the room. Invite students to use the model to identify and label the different bones of the body. If desired, make copies of the skeleton patterns for students to cut out and assemble for their own use.

★ LIFE-SIZE SKELETONS

Motivate students to show what they know about their bones with these life-sized skeletons! First have them trace around each other's body on lengths of bulletin-board paper. Then ask students to cut out their body outlines. Distribute copies of the Mr. Skeleton patterns (pages 109–113) for them to cut out and glue in the appropriate areas of their body outline. (The patterns are just about the right size for most kindergartners, but they may need to be enlarged for older or larger students.) Display the completed skeletons around the room for all to enjoy.

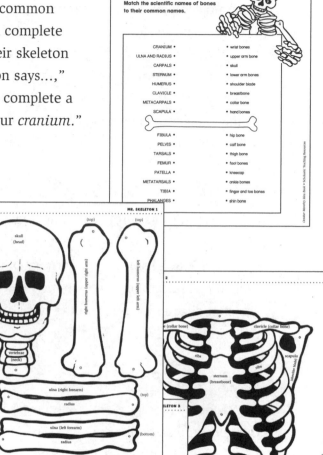

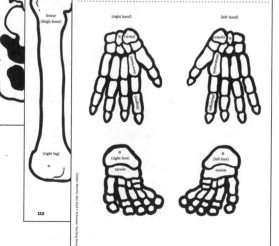

FLASHLIGHT X-RAY

After a discussion about the human skeleton, let students view a part of their own skeleton with this intriguing activity. To begin, darken the room and turn on a flashlight. Then invite students to take turns holding the palm of their hand over the light of the flashlight. If they look carefully, they'll be able to see the bones in their hand and the joints connecting their fingers. Ask students to draw pictures of their observations.

ALL ABOUT BONES

Have students ever broken a bone? Do they know where their "funny bone" is? Do they know what the phrase "No bones about it" means? Invite students to write about their experiences with broken or bruised bones and bone-related phrases. Then create a skeleton character similar to the one shown here to display on a bulletin board. Post students' writing and add a title.

BONY MATH

Tell students that as a baby, they had 300 bones. But by the time they become an adult, they will have only 206 bones. Ask them to calculate the difference in the bone count of a baby and adult. Then explain that as students grow, many of their bones fuse together, resulting in fewer bones by the time they are fully grown. Share the following adult bone counts with students, then have them use the numbers to create and solve a variety of math problems.

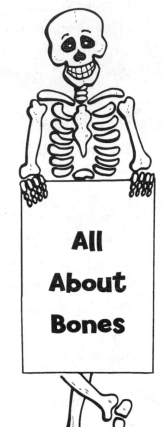

All About Bones

Each arm has 3 bones.

Each hand has 27 bones.

Each leg has 4 bones.

Each foot has 26 bones.

The skull has 29 bones.

The spine has 26 bones.

The chest has 25 bones.

Hello, Bones!

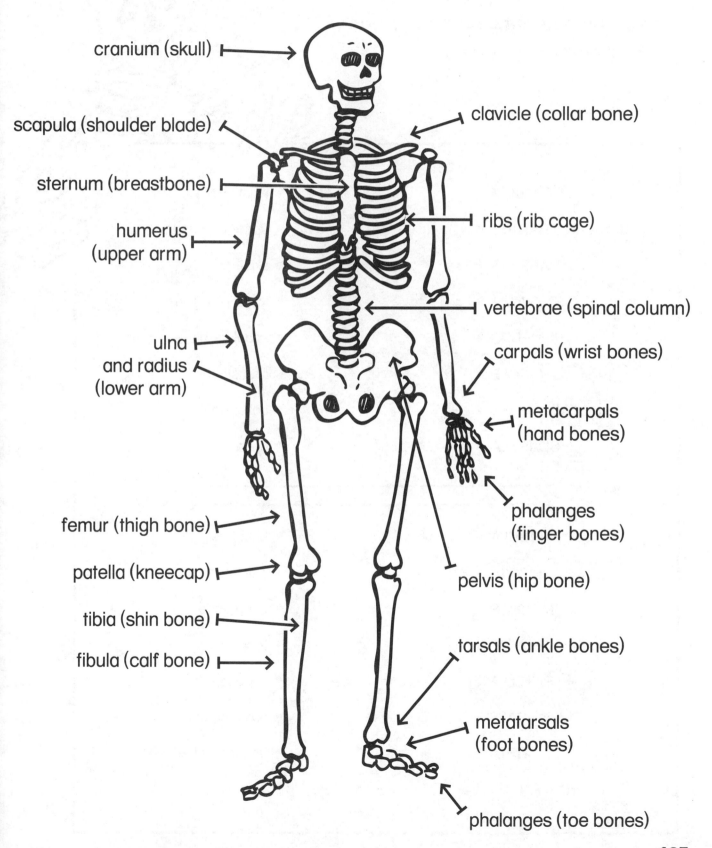

cranium (skull)

scapula (shoulder blade)

sternum (breastbone)

humerus
(upper arm)

ulna
and radius
(lower arm)

femur (thigh bone)

patella (kneecap)

tibia (shin bone)

fibula (calf bone)

clavicle (collar bone)

ribs (rib cage)

vertebrae (spinal column)

carpals (wrist bones)

metacarpals
(hand bones)

phalanges
(finger bones)

pelvis (hip bone)

tarsals (ankle bones)

metatarsals
(foot bones)

phalanges (toe bones)

Skeleton Match

Match the scientific names of bones to their common names.

CRANIUM • • wrist bones

ULNA AND RADIUS • • upper arm bone

CARPALS • • skull

STERNUM • • lower arm bones

HUMERUS • • shoulder blade

CLAVICLE • • breastbone

METACARPALS • • collar bone

SCAPULA • • hand bones

FIBULA • • hip bone

PELVIS • • calf bone

TARSALS • • thigh bone

FEMUR • • foot bones

PATELLA • • kneecap

METATARSALS • • ankle bones

TIBIA • • finger and toe bones

PHALANGES • • shin bone

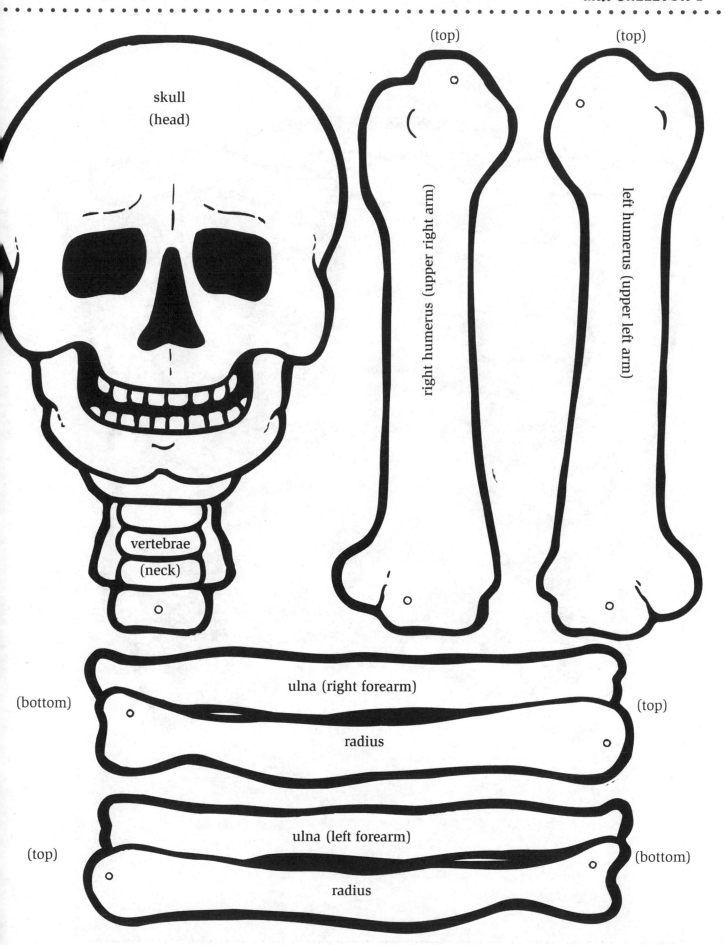

skull
(head)

(top)

(top)

right humerus (upper right arm)

left humerus (upper left arm)

vertebrae
(neck)

(bottom)

ulna (right forearm)

(top)

radius

(top)

ulna (left forearm)

(bottom)

radius

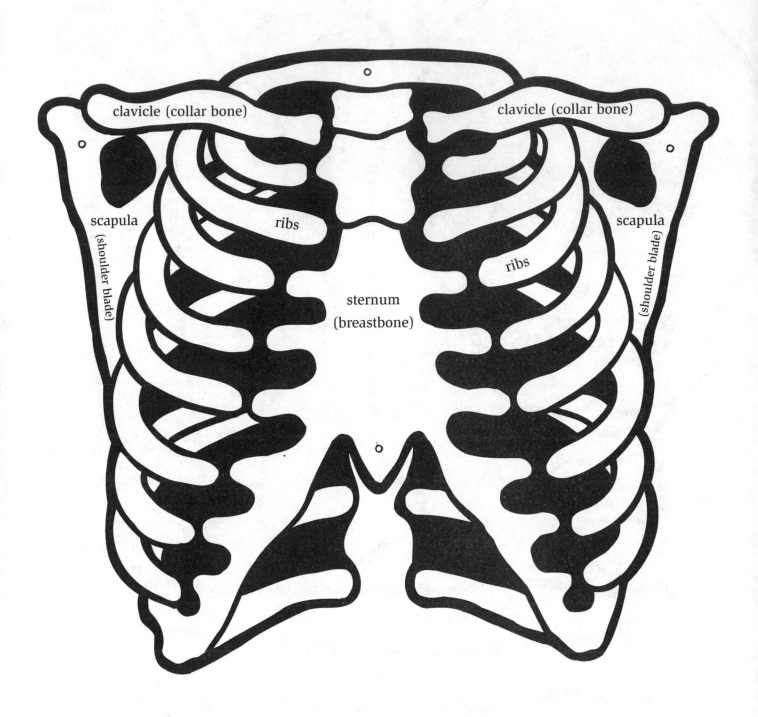

clavicle (collar bone)

clavicle (collar bone)

scapula

scapula

(shoulder blade)

(shoulder blade)

ribs

ribs

sternum
(breastbone)

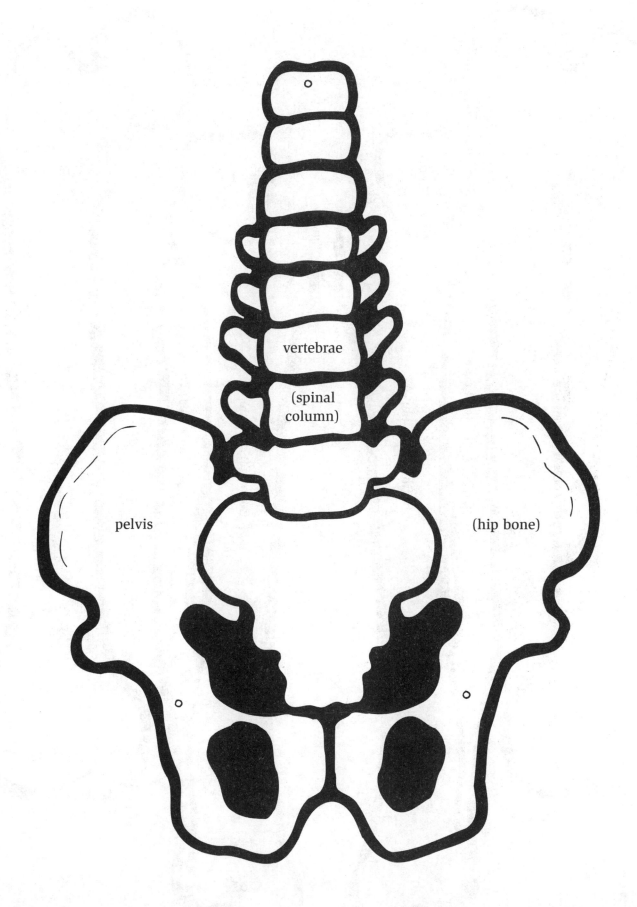

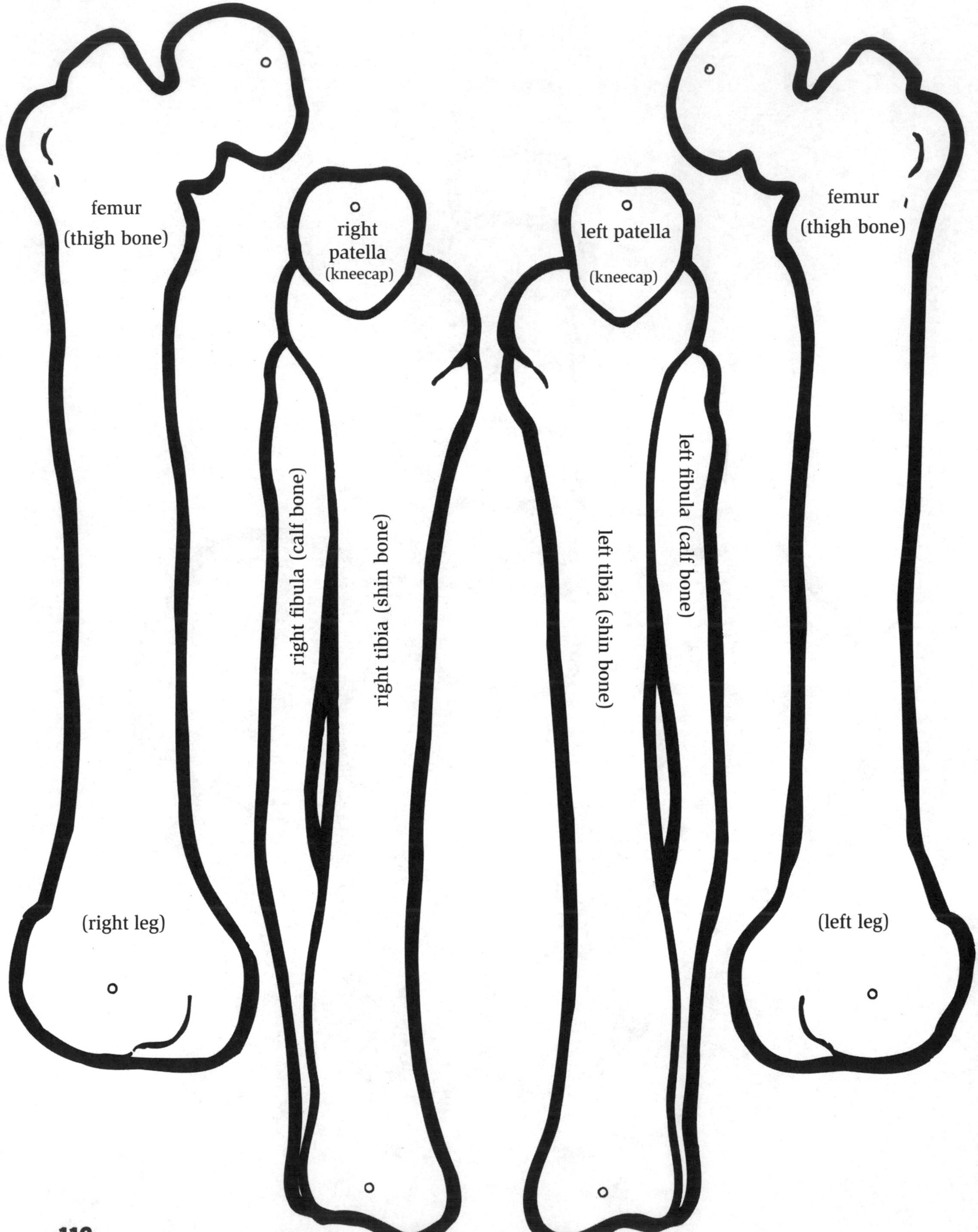

femur
(thigh bone)

right
patella
(kneecap)

left patella

(kneecap)

femur
(thigh bone)

right fibula (calf bone)

right tibia (shin bone)

left tibia (shin bone)

left fibula (calf bone)

(right leg)

(left leg)

October Monthly Idea Book © Scholastic Teaching Resources

(right hand)

(left hand)

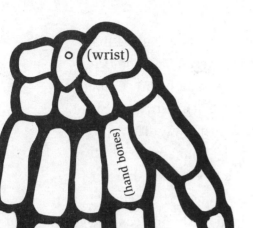

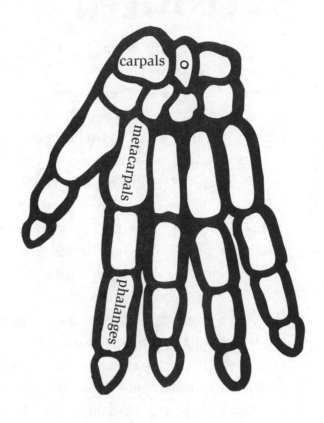

(wrist)

(hand bones)

(fingers)

carpals

metacarpals

phalanges

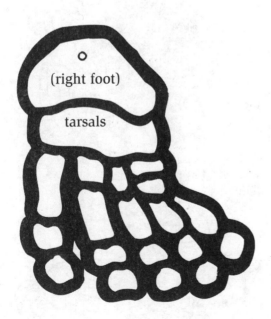

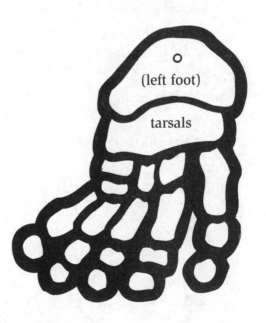

(right foot)

tarsals

(left foot)

tarsals

HALLOWEEN

No one knows exactly when Halloween was first celebrated. Many believe the ancient Druids of England were the first to recognize this special day. The Druids observed New Year's Day on November 1st. This made the night before, October 31, their New Year's Eve. They believed that on this night, evil spirits were called forth to visit the earth. The Druids lit great fires to scare them away. They also dressed as ghosts and goblins in hopes of escaping the night unharmed.

Eventually, Christians began to celebrate All Hallow's Day at the same time. This was a day on which they honored the saints of the Church. The night before, All Hallow's Eve (or Halloween), people dressed in masks and costumes meant to represent the saints. It was their duty to lead the spirits of the dead out of town before the next day's celebration.

After the Romans conquered Britain, harvest festivals became part of the Halloween celebrations. In Scotland, farmers carried torches through fields in hopes of a good crop for the next year and to frighten away evil spirits that might be hiding in the orchards and pastures. The Irish hollowed out and carved potatoes and turnips, then lit candles inside the shells to scare away evil spirits.

Halloween has changed throughout the years. Today, it is a favorite occasion of many children—a time to dress up in costumes, play pretend, enjoy some light-hearted scares, collect treats, and enjoy the carnival-like atmosphere of the event. To prepare students for a wonderful Halloween, review safety rules with them first, then use the activities in this unit to enhance their experience.

Suggested Activities

★ MASKS AROUND THE WORLD

Throughout the history of the world, masks have played an important role in celebrations, death ceremonies, and theatrical presentations. Masks might cover part of the face or the entire face and can be made from a variety of materials, including wood, paper, and gold. With masks also being a large part of the fun of Halloween, take some time to share with students some interesting information about masks from other parts of the world.

Africa: Masks are an important and respected part of many African ceremonies—they are often believed to contain great powers. Dancers might wear beautiful masks representing a particular spirit or animal. Invite students to research African cultures and find pictures of ceremonial masks. If desired, have them make paper-bag animal masks.

Alaska: Inuit men carve masks from driftwood to use in ceremonial dances, which usually tell a story. Often, these masks are decorated with eagle feathers, sealskin, and animal fur and represent spirits said to bring luck in fishing and hunting. The women carve small finger masks that they move to the music during ceremonial dances. Invite students to make finger masks from the patterns on pages 121.

Egypt: To make death masks, the Egyptians took wax impressions of the deceased's face and then covered them with sheets of gold. This ritual was believed to protect the deceased from evil spirits. Find pictures of King Tutankhamen's treasures, including his death mask, to share with students.

Greece: Early Greeks wore animal masks to worship their gods. Later, actors began to use masks on stage. An actor could play several roles simply by changing masks, which often held small megaphones to help the audience hear the actor speak. Greek theatrical masks usually fell into two categories: tragedy and comedy. Ask students to create masks to use as props when they act out skits or familiar stories, such as fairy tales.

Mexico and South America: The ancient people of Mexico and South America made beautiful relief masks from thin sheets of gold. Masks were usually used in story-telling and for entertainment. Invite students to cover a tagboard mask with heavy-duty aluminum foil and then etch designs in the foil with a blunt pencil point. Or, to help students learn Spanish color words, have them color tagboard copies of the Mexican mask (page 122) as indicated. Add a large craft-stick handle to the completed mask.

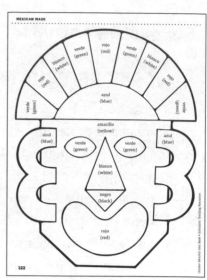

North America: The Iroquois of North America carved masks from living trees, which kept the masks "alive" and preserved their magical powers. The masks were painted red if cut in the morning and black if cut later in the day. These "false faces" had metal-rimmed eyes that glowed in the light of the campfire and horsetail hair for wigs. Invite students to research, describe, and draw masks that the Iroquois might have made.

★ MAKE-YOUR-OWN MASK

What kind of mask would students make to represent something about themselves or their beliefs? Provide a choice of the mask patterns on pages 123–124 (copied onto tagboard), along with an assortment of craft materials for students to use in decorating their masks. When finished, help them attach yarn ties to each side of their mask.

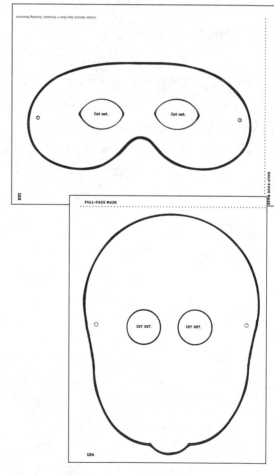

★ IT'S PUMPKIN TIME!

Pumpkins and Halloween go hand-in-hand. As students gear up for the big day, introduce them to the wonders of pumpkins. First, explain that pumpkins are a popular Halloween sight—whether seen ripening in a pumpkin patch, as the centerpiece of fall table settings, or adorning doorsteps in the form of jack-o'-lanterns. Then present a pumpkin for students to explore. Have them share observations, using sensory descriptions of the different attributes of the pumpkin. After examining its exterior, cut open the pumpkin and let students examine the inside. What do they see? How does the interior feel? Smell? Taste? Finally, work with students to carve a face in the pumpkin to make a class jack-o'-lantern. Later, distribute copies of the pumpkin stationery (page 125) and book cover (page 126) for students to use for their Halloween- and pumpkin-related writing.

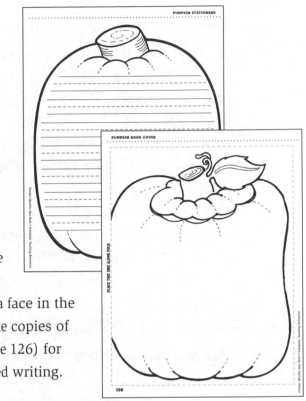

★ PUMPKIN PLANTS

Save the seeds from your jack-o'-lantern to plant later in the year. Dry the pumpkin seeds on waxed paper, then store in an airtight container until spring arrives. At that time, give students a plastic cup or pint-sized milk carton (with the top trimmed off) to use as a planter. Have them fill the planter with soil, plant a few pumpkin seeds, and set the planter on a windowsill or in another sunny area. Remind students to care for their plants, checking that the soil is kept slightly moist. When the seeds sprout, students can take their plants home to share with their family.

★ PUMPKIN MUNCHIES

Roast some pumpkin seeds for a munchy snack! Have students help separate seeds from the pumpkin pulp. Wash the seeds and place on a greased cookie sheet. Sprinkle with a little sea salt, then roast in an oven at 350°F. Remove the seeds when they turn brown (about 20 minutes), and cool before serving. For an instant math activity, make up problems for students to solve with the seeds. Then invite them to enjoy the seeds for a light snack.

★ FOUR-SIDED PUMPKIN

Invite students to explore emotions with this easy-to-make project. Beforehand, discuss the various emotions they might experience on Halloween, for example, happiness, fear, surprise, and sadness. Then distribute copies of the four-sided pumpkin pattern (page 127) for students to cut out. Ask them to draw a face that represents a different emotion on each side of the pumpkin. When finished, help them fold each side up toward the center and staple the tops together. Invite students to share their pumpkins with the class, telling about each face and what might cause them to experience the emotion it depicts.

★ WHAT HALLOWEEN MEANS TO ME

Halloween means different things to different people. Some enjoy the costumes and treats, others the silly and sometimes frightful sights, and still others are happy because the day signals that fall has arrived. Invite students to create an acrostic poem, using the letters in "Halloween" to describe what it means to them. Copy and distribute page 128 for students to use for their poems. As they write, instruct them to use a word at the beginning of each line that starts with the letter on the left. Encourage students to share their completed poems in small groups.

★ HALLOWEEN LEARNING ACTIVITIES

It's easy to make Halloween a time for learning fun. Following are activities you can use to teach and reinforce a variety of skills.

Word Find

Distribute a copy of the Halloween Word Find (page 129) to students and explain that the word bank contains words associated with Halloween. Ask them to find and circle those words in their word-find puzzle. Then have them respond to the writing prompt at the bottom of the page.

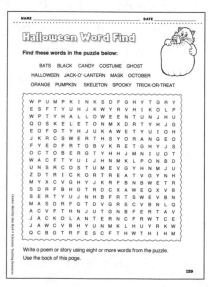

Where Is Cat's Jack-o'-Lantern?

For this game, color, cut out, and glue pages 130 and 131 together to make the game board. Then prepare task cards for the skill you'd like students to practice, such as reading sight words or solving simple math problems. (Where appropriate, write answers on the back of the cards or prepare an answer key to make the game self-checking.) Laminate the game board and task cards for durability. Invite pairs or small groups of students to play the game, as follows:

1. Place a marker on Start. Shuffle the cards and stack them nearby.

2. Toss a penny. If it lands on heads, move one space. If tails, move two spaces.

3. Move your marker. Follow any directions on the space. Otherwise, take a card and perform the task.

4. Check your answer, or ask other players if they agree with your response. If so, leave your marker on the space. If not, move your marker back.

5. Continue play, taking turns until a player reaches Finish. That player wins the game.

★ FLYING FACT BAT

Ask students to use sources, such as the Internet and nonfiction library books, to research bats. Have them write some of their favorite bat facts on a copy of the bat pattern (page 132) and then cut out the pattern. Help students fold the bat body up and the wings out, as shown. Then add a length of yarn to suspend the bats around the room. Invite students to share the information on their bat with the class.

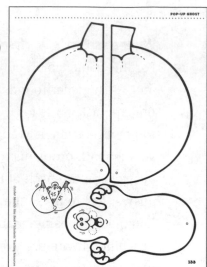

POP-UP GHOST

These hinged pumpkins hide a cute ghost inside. To assemble, cut out construction-paper copies of the pumpkin and ghost patterns on page 133. (Make as many copies as you need for the skill you plan to teach.) Program the pumpkin with the skill you want to teach and write the answer on the ghost. Use a brass fastener to attach the ghost to the pumpkin pieces, as shown. To use, students read the task, give their response, then open the pumpkin so that the ghost "pops" up with the answer. If desired, have students make their own pop-up ghosts. They might write clues about a mystery object on the pumpkin and draw the object on the ghost. Or, they might write a riddle on the pumpkin and the answer on the ghost.

GHOST WHEEL

Use the ghost wheel patterns on pages 134–135 to reinforce math skills and more. To prepare, write a problem in each of the large boxes (outlined in gray). Write the answer in the small box directly opposite each problem on the left. Cut out the ghost, pumpkin, and wheel. Then carefully cut out the "windows" on the ghost. Use one brass fastener to attach the wheel to the ghost and another to attach the pumpkin, as shown. To use, students turn to the wheel so that a problem appears in the right window. They solve the problem and then slide the pumpkin away from the left window to check their answer.

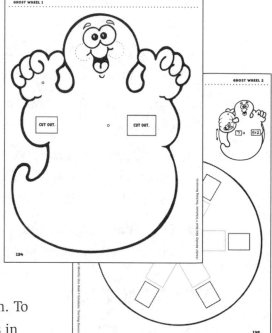

CAT PAGE FRAMER

To display students' spooky stories or Halloween art, give them the cat page-framer patterns (page 136) to color and cut out. Have them mount their page on a 9- by 12-inch sheet of black or orange construction paper. Then have them glue the cat patterns to the edges of the paper.

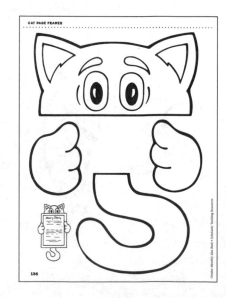

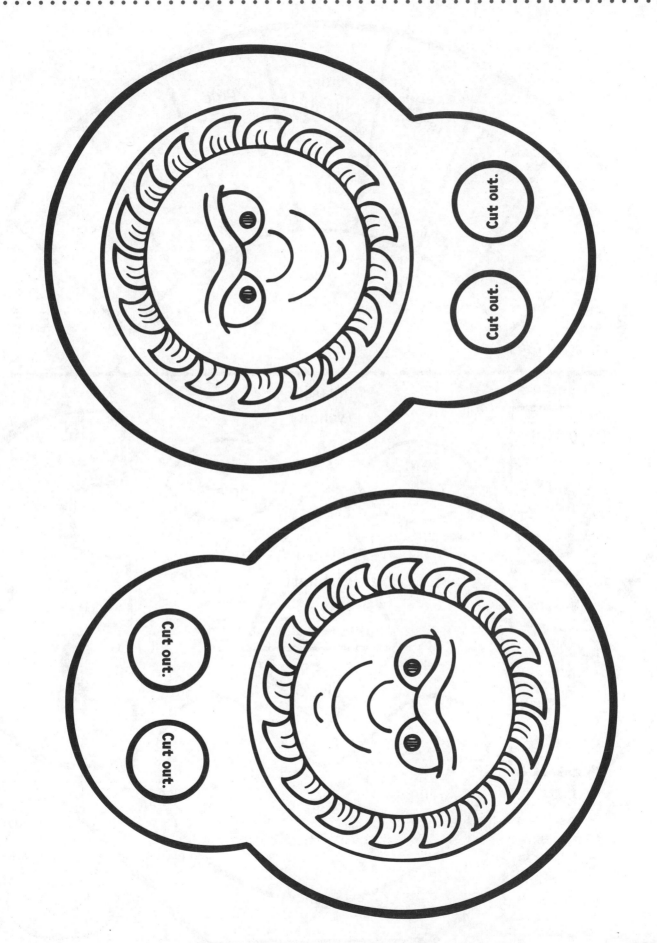

Cut out.

Cut out.

Cut out.

Cut out.

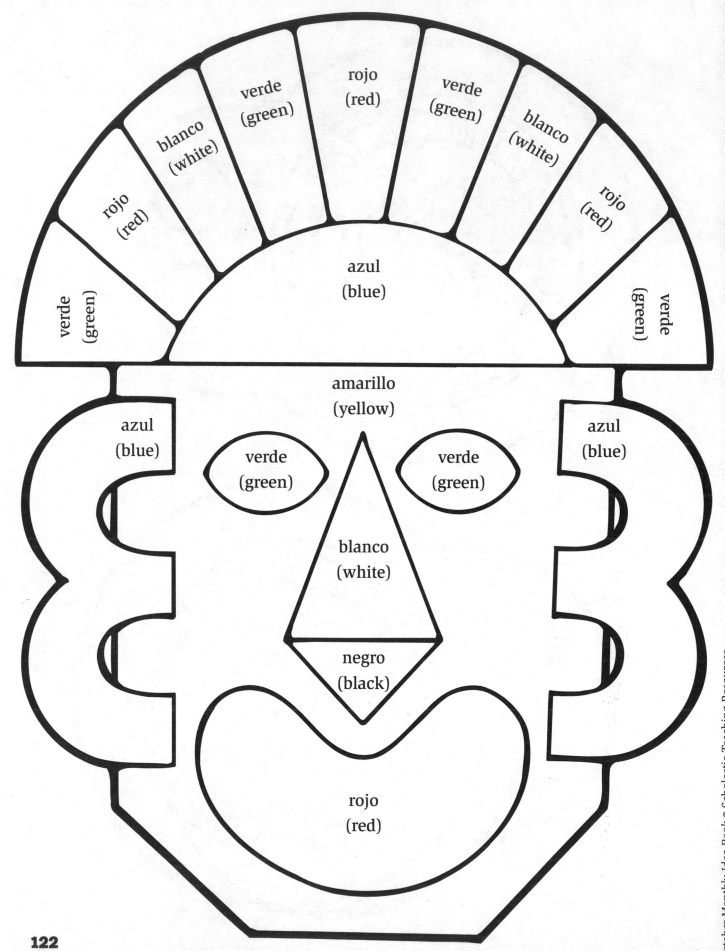

October Monthly Idea Book © Scholastic Teaching Resources

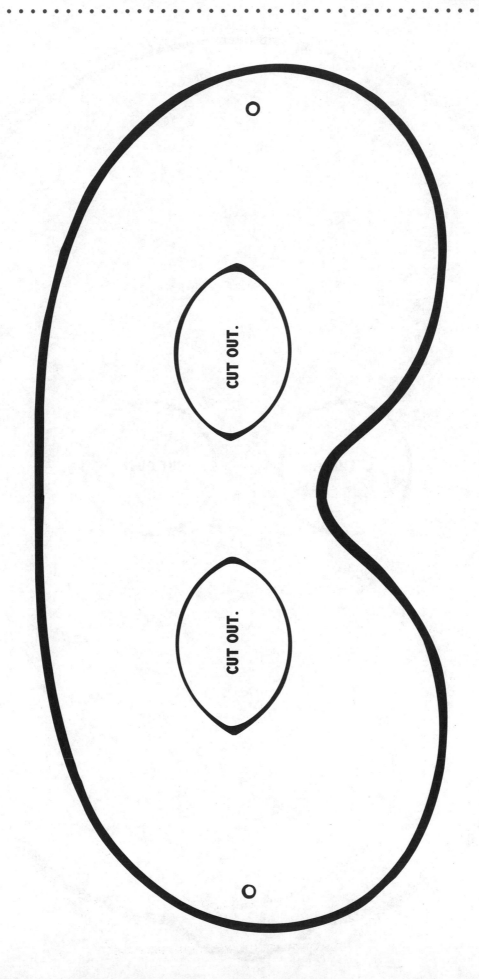

CUT OUT.

CUT OUT.

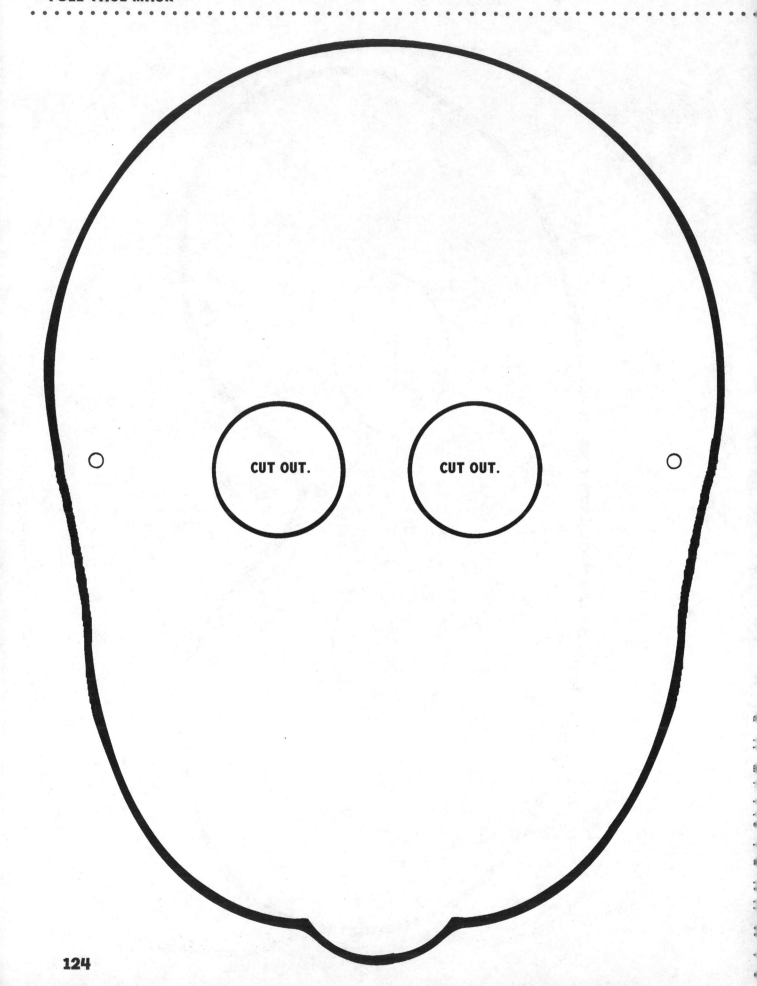

CUT OUT.

CUT OUT.

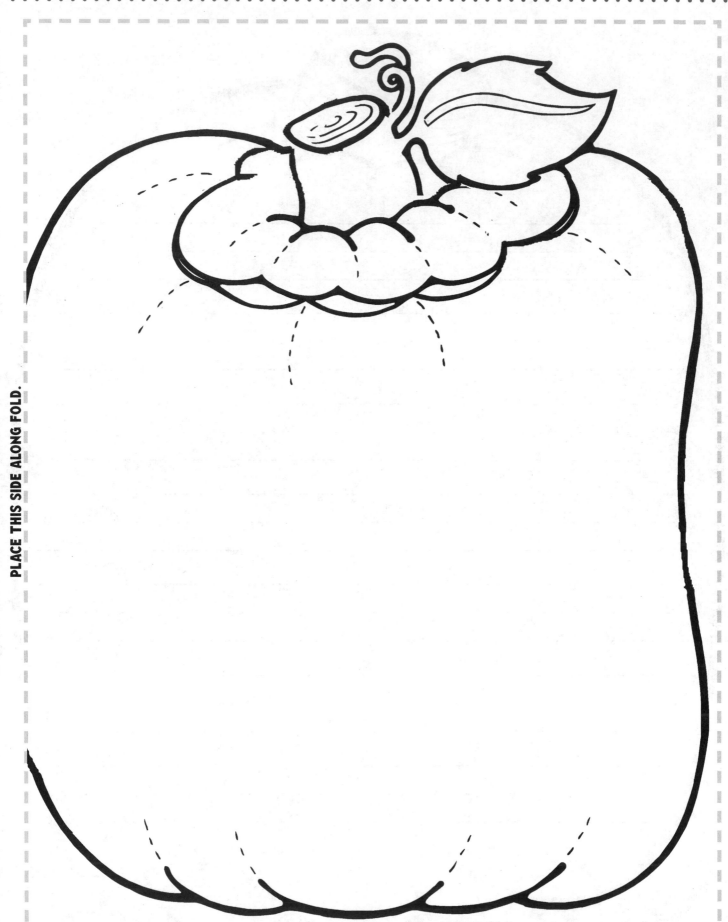

PLACE THIS SIDE ALONG FOLD.

October Monthly Idea Book © Scholastic Teaching Resources

Halloween Acrostic

H ——————————————————————————————————

A ——————————————————————————————————

L ——————————————————————————————————

L ——————————————————————————————————

O ——————————————————————————————————

W ——————————————————————————————————

E ——————————————————————————————————

E ——————————————————————————————————

N ——————————————————————————————————

Halloween Word Find

Find these words in the puzzle below:

BATS   BLACK   CANDY   COSTUME   GHOST

HALLOWEEN   JACK-O'-LANTERN   MASK   OCTOBER

ORANGE   PUMPKIN   SKELETON   SPOOKY   TRICK-OR-TREAT

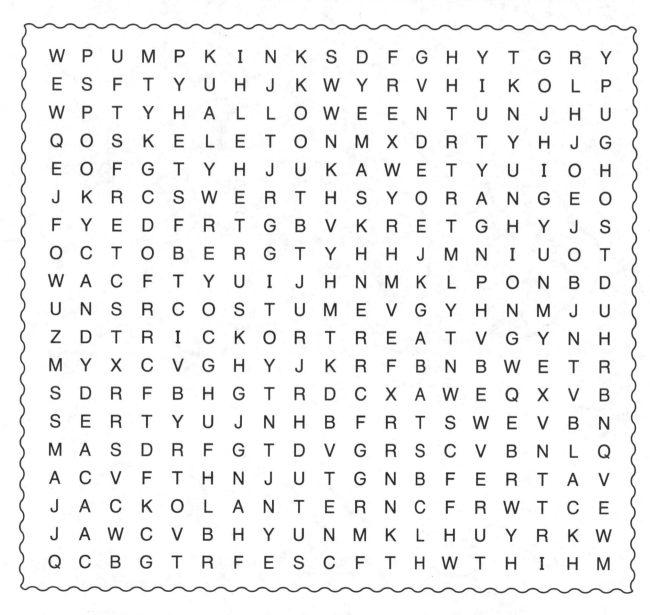

```
W P U M P K I N K S D F G H Y T G R Y
E S F T Y U H J K W Y R V H I K O L P
W P T Y H A L L O W E E N T U N J H U
Q O S K E L E T O N M X D R T Y H J G
E O F G T Y H J U K A W E T Y U I O H
J K R C S W E R T H S Y O R A N G E O
F Y E D F R T G B V K R E T G H Y J S
O C T O B E R G T Y H H J M N I U O T
W A C F T Y U I J H N M K L P O N B D
U N S R C O S T U M E V G Y H N M J U
Z D T R I C K O R T R E A T V G Y N H
M Y X C V G H Y J K R F B N B W E T R
S D R F B H G T R D C X A W E Q X V B
S E R T Y U J N H B F R T S W E V B N
M A S D R F G T D V G R S C V B N L Q
A C V F T H N J U T G N B F E R T A V
J A C K O L A N T E R N C F R W T C E
J A W C V B H Y U N M K L H U Y R K W
Q C B G T R F E S C F T H W T H I H M
```

Write a poem or story using eight or more words from the puzzle.

Use the back of this page.

Where Is Cat's Jack-o'-Lantern?

Start

1.
2.
3.
14.
16. Move ahead 1 space.
15.
17.
18.
19.
20.
21.
22.
23. Move back 3 spaces.

PLACE THIS SIDE ALONG FOLD.

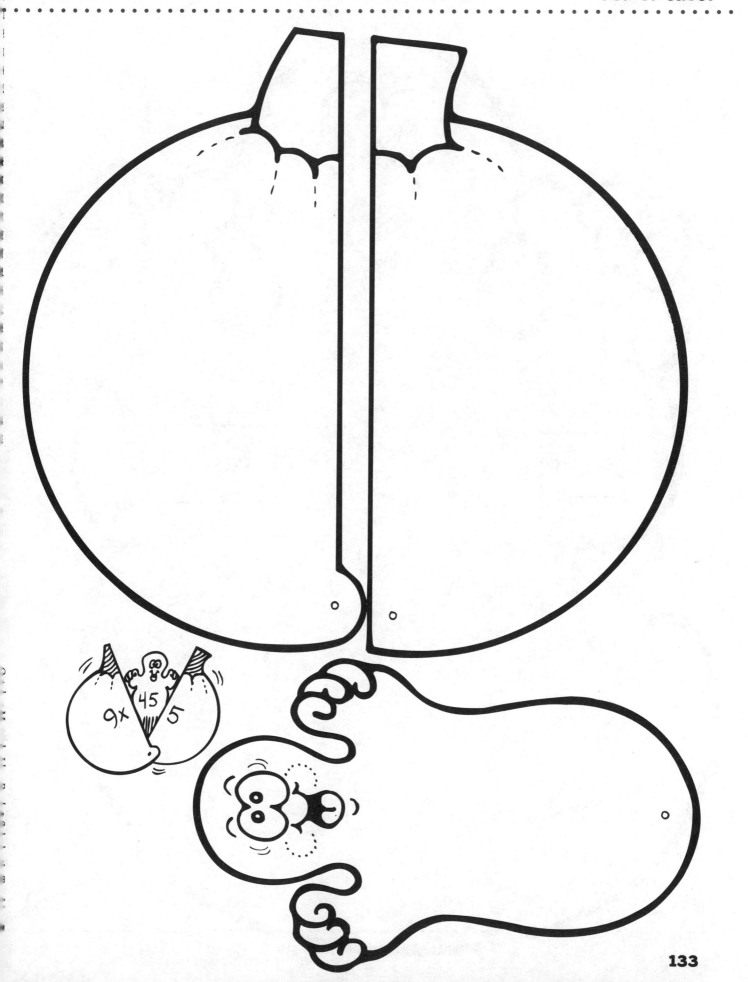

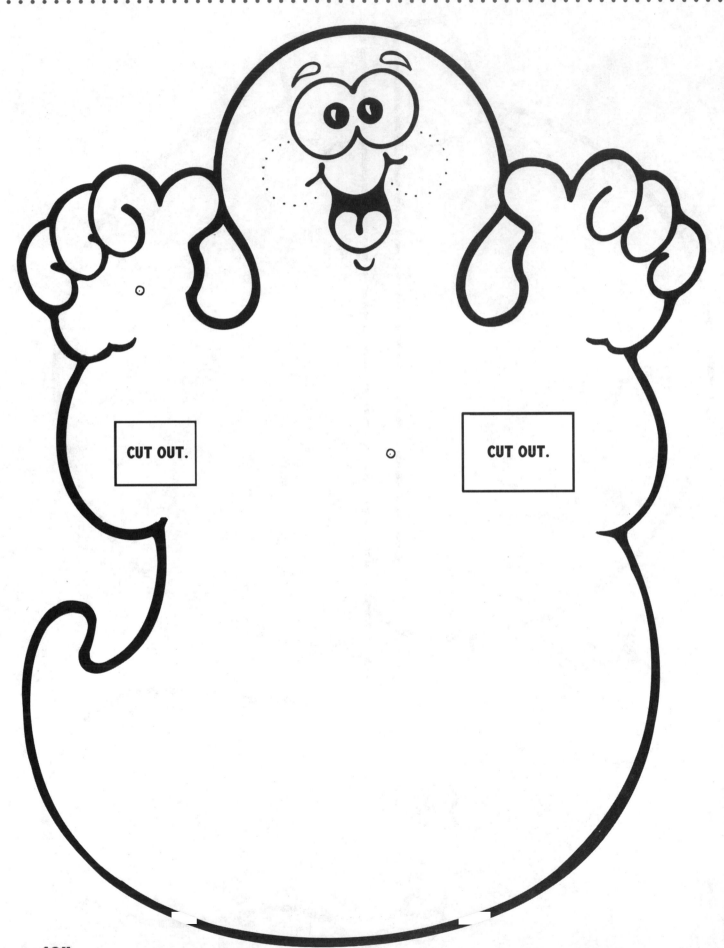

CUT OUT.

CUT OUT.

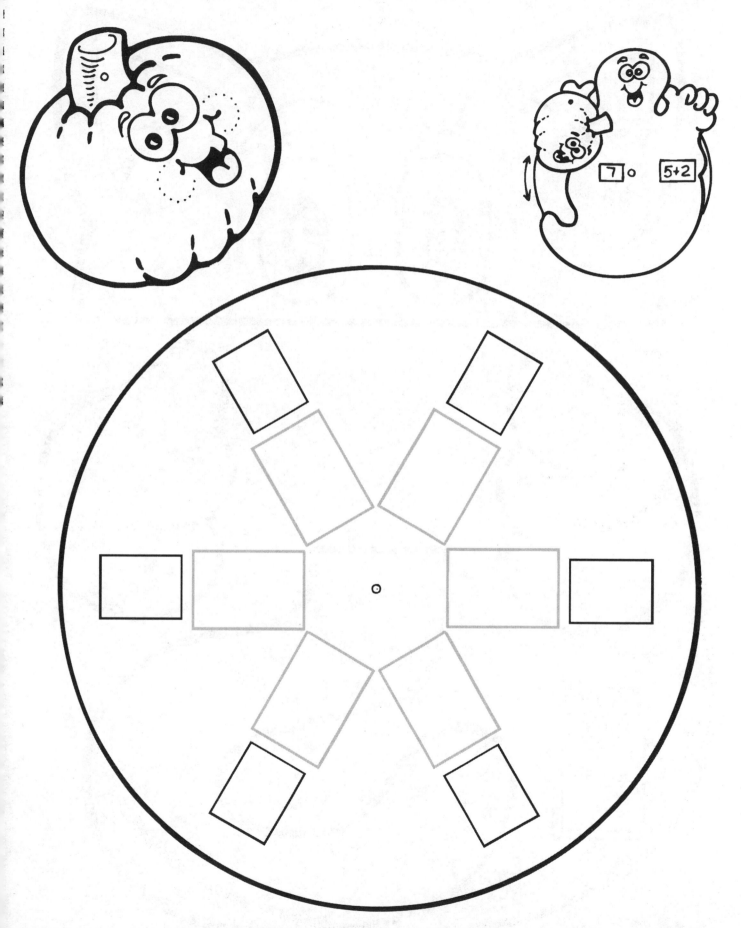

Scary Story

AWARDS, INCENTIVES, AND MORE

Getting Started

Make several photocopies of the reproducibles on pages 139 through 143. Giving out the bookmarks, pencil toppers, notes, and certificates will show students your enthusiasm for their efforts and achievements. Plus, bookmarks and pencil toppers are a fun treat for students celebrating birthdays.

- Provide materials for decorating, including markers, color pencils, and stickers.

- Encourage students to bring home their creations to share and celebrate with family members.

★ BOOKMARKS

1. Photocopy onto tagboard and cut apart.

2. For more fanfare, punch a hole on one end and tie on a length of colorful ribbon or yarn.

★ PENCIL TOPPERS

1. Photocopy onto tagboard and cut out.

2. Use an art knife to cut through the Xs.

3. Slide a pencil through the Xs as shown.

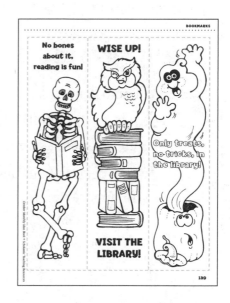

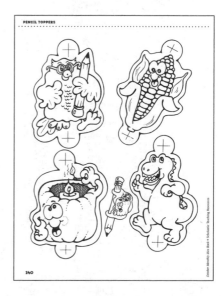

SEND-HOME NOTES

1. Photocopy and cut apart.

2. Record the child's name and the date.

3. Add your signature.

4. Add more details about the student's day on the back of the note.

 CERTIFICATES

1. Photocopy.

2. Record the child's name and other information, as directed.

3. Add details about the child's achievement (if applicable), then add your signature and the date.

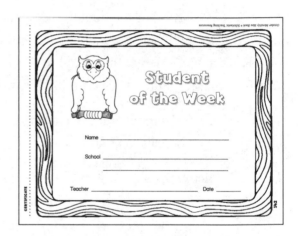

No bones about it, reading is fun!

WISE UP!

VISIT THE LIBRARY!

Only treats, no tricks, in the library!

_____
Student's Name

has something to crow about! _____

_____

_____   _____
Teacher   Date

_____
Student's Name

Hoot, hoot, hooray!

You had a great day!

_____   _____
Teacher   Date

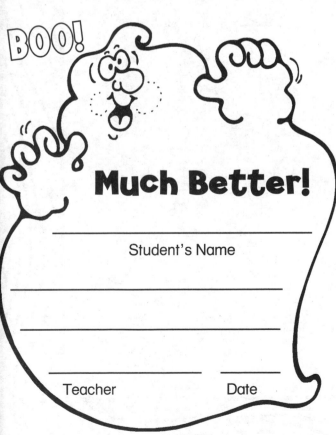

BOO!

Much Better!

_____
Student's Name

_____

_____

_____   _____
Teacher   Date

_____
Student's Name

was a "huge" success today!

_____
Date

_____
Teacher

Student of the Week

Name

School

Teacher

Date

Certificate of Achievement

presented to

Name

in recognition of

Teacher

Date

Columbus Word Find, page 49

```
D V B H Y U J K O L M N H G V B H F R T Y
C O L U M B U S S E R T G Y H U J K I L P
W E R T G Y H P D C V B Q S E R T Y U I P
Z C V F G T H A S W R T U F G H Y U J M N
C F G R T B N I F R T Y E D R Y H J P S Q
S C V B G F D N R T Y H E C O L K I I N G
A M E T Y F E B C D R W N Q X C V T N H U
N E S A N T A M A R I A I F V B G T T D R
S W E T Y G H U I J K Y S D R T Y E A V F
B G T Y U J H F G T V B A M E R I C A T U
W E R T G D V F H F T R B W T Y U P I B N
Q U E F T G H K I N G F E R D I N A N D R
D C V G H B G F V F D S L S R T G Y T R E
D N E W W O R L D F T E L F R T Y G F R E
F B V C D S A N S A L V A D O R F T Y H U
S D F G T Y H U J N B V C X Z D R T G D R
S R V B N M K J G F D N I Ñ A S E F Y H O
```

Halloween Word Find, page 129

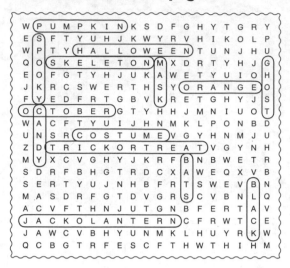

```
W P U M P K I N K S D F G H Y T G R Y
E S F T Y U H J K W Y R V H I K O L P
W P T Y H A L L O W E E N T U N J H U
Q O S K E L E T O N M X D R T Y H J G
E O F G T Y H J U K A W E T Y U I O H
J K R C S W E R T H S Y O R A N G E O
F Y E D F R T G B V K R E T G H Y J S
O C T O B E R G T Y H H J M N I U O T
W A C F T Y U I J H N M K L P O N B D
U N S R C O S T U M E V G Y H N M J U
Z D T R I C K O R T R E A T V G Y N H
M Y X C V G H Y J K R F B N B W E T R
S D R F B H G T R D C X A W E Q X V B
S E R T Y U J N H B F R T S W E V B N
M A S D R F G T D V G R S C V B N L Q
A C V F T H N J U T G N B F E R T A C
J A C K O L A N T E R N C F R W T C K
J A W C V B N J N M K L H U Y R K W
Q C B G T R F E S C F T H W T H I H M
```

Skeleton Match, page 108

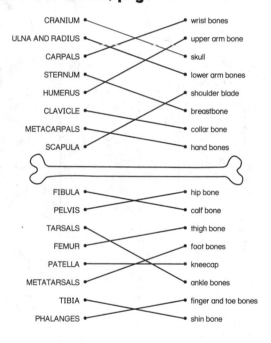

CRANIUM — skull
ULNA AND RADIUS — lower arm bones
CARPALS — wrist bones
STERNUM — breastbone
HUMERUS — upper arm bone
CLAVICLE — collar bone
METACARPALS — hand bones
SCAPULA — shoulder blade

FIBULA — calf bone
PELVIS — hip bone
TARSALS — ankle bones
FEMUR — thigh bone
PATELLA — kneecap
METATARSALS — foot bones
TIBIA — shin bone
PHALANGES — finger and toe bones